THE CONCISE

BIRDS

OF BRITAIN AND EUROPE

An Illustrated Checklist

by
Hermann Heinzel

Date _____

Name _____

Address _____

_____

_____

HODDER AND STOUGHTON
LONDON SYDNEY AUCKLAND TORONTO

£2.95
net

Contents

A **Domino Books** production

Compiled and painted by Hermann Heinzel

Filmset by Ace Filmsetting, Frome
Colour reproduction by Adroit PhotoLitho, Birmingham
Printed and bound in Spain by Heraclio Fournier, Vitoria

© in text and illustration Hermann Heinzel 1985

ISBN 0 340 37213 3

First published in Great Britain by Hodder & Stoughton Ltd.

Introduction

This book started off as something I had wanted myself since I started bird-watching: a proper printed, bound list of all the birds in Europe, with room to note what I had seen.

Something not too bulky to carry comfortably around. Much slimmer and lighter than the book I designed and painted 15 years ago, with text and maps by Richard Fitter and John Parslow. That was (still is) *The Birds of Britain and Europe with North Africa and the Middle East* – at 336 pages, as long as its title!

But then I thought: why not colour pictures of all the birds? And give them all distribution maps? So it has (I hope) ended up an ultra-compact, ultra-lightweight bird guide too, with a reminder of what each species look like and of how in some species females, winter plumages or the more distinct regional subspecies, differ. True, some species such as the warblers are small. But these are birds which only an experienced birdwatcher can distinguish in practice anyway.

The following two pages show how the book works. I omitted juveniles, which would have cluttered and confused the design, but included symbols to indicate each bird's status and frequency in Britain and Ireland.

I hope other birdwatchers may find it useful too. To beginners I would say: don't hesitate to scribble notes all over it. It is meant to be used, and there is nothing in bird study so useful and rewarding as keeping notes, one's own personal record of a season, a trip, a year, or a lifetime. When did the Swifts come last year – and leave? What birds have we seen on this holiday? Which British thrushes have we still to see? When did I first hear a cuckoo last year, or see a Brambling? The ideal is even to keep a separate record for each year.

Britain is not only a world headquarters of ornithological studies and bird conservation: it is also among the most varied regions of Europe for habitat and birdlife. You also have in the Royal Society for the Protection of Birds the world's largest, and surely the best, bird club and protection society, which sends its members an admirable magazine. Its address is The Lodge, Sandy, Bedfordshire. Among my best memories have been watching waders on East Anglian mudflats, my first Scottish Crossbill in a wood above Loch Affric. Red Grouse on a rainy day in Perthshire, Temminck's and Little Stints near Chichester, Manx Shearwaters, Fulmars and Choughs on Bardsey Island off the Welsh coast. Wonderful times, but I wish now that I had kept notes.

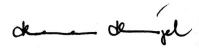

A single bird, with no sex symbol, indicates a species in which the male (♂) and female (♀) are for practical purposes identical in the field. The picture is of a typical adult male in breeding plumage – except in the case of visitors usually seen in Europe in their winter plumage, which is then illustrated and captioned as such.

A single bird with a male symbol is a species in which the female does differ but would be distinguishable from the male only by an experienced ornithologist: she is invariably duller in colour.

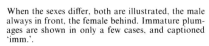

When the sexes differ, both are illustrated, the male always in front, the female behind. Immature plumages are shown in only a few cases, and captioned 'imm.'.

Some species show distinct regional differences. These subspecies are illustrated (males only, the females do not generally differ regionally) and named. Thus *Passer domesticus* is the common House Sparrow, with a distinct southern race is *P. domesticus italiae*.

♂ *italiae*

Reeve

Ruff

Colour phases or 'morphs' occur in many species, such as here in the Ruff and in many raptors. Typical examples are given with their own 'ticker boxes'. Not illustrated are albinos or melanistic (black) mutations except in the Montagu's Harrier, Partridge and Snipe.

A small bird in flight shows some typical pattern of wing, tail, rump or belly which is useful for identification but not visible in the standing bird.

When the winter plumage of a species differs sharply from the breeding (summer) plumage, this is usually illustrated behind, and captioned with a W.

W

♂ S

♂ W

Ptarmigan and Willow Grouse are examples of birds with three annual plumages: winter, summer and intermediate. We show the two extremes. Many drakes also undergo a plumage change after breeding, often immediately, while the ducks are still on the nest. These 'eclipse' plumages are not shown, as the drakes then tend to become much duller, and to resemble the females so that only an experienced ornithologist can distinguish them. They also become secretive in their behaviour.

	FINCHES: *Fringillidae*	12:8 – 20:2

A blue strip always indicates the start of a new Family.

After the English and scientific names of the Family are given first the numbers of species in the Family recorded in Britain and Ireland, and then the same for all Europe including the British Isles. In each case the first figure is the number of breeding species and regular visitors, and the second figure (after the : sign) is the number of irregular visitors or accidentals. Thus in Britain and Ireland there are 12 regular Finch species and 8 accidentals, and throughout Europe 20 and 2.

☐ **BLACK REDSTART**	S P w ○	
Phoenicurus ochruros Originally a mountain or hill bird, colonising Britain recently. Now *c.* 30 breeding pairs, in towns.		

You can tick this box as a personal record.

Some distinctive or interesting characters.

☐ *Ph. o. aterrimus*	—	Portugal SC Spain

Fainter boxes are used for subspecies, colour phases or 'morphs'.

After the names of each species are given its British frequency/status symbols (see below) and a distribution map. Sometimes arrows beside the map, pointing up or down, indicate a bird whose overall European population is increasing (↑) or decreasing (↓): doubled arrows (↑↑, ↓↓), sharply so. In the map breeding species is shown in bright red and non-breeding areas in blue. The region in which a named subspecies is found is included in the map and noted after its symbols.

The following symbols indicate the frequence and status of each species as it occurs in Britain and Ireland. No symbols (—) indicates a bird not found in Britain.

● common and widely distributed breeding bird

● uncommon or only locally common breeding bird

○ a rare or very local breeding bird

▲ frequent and widely occurring non-breeding visitor

▲ uncommon or local non-breeding visitor

△ a rare though regular visitor, in small numbers

┌ principal populations
│ ┌ subsidiary populations

R r resident all year round, though may migrate inside Britain

S s summer visitor

P p passage migrant, stopping on its migration route over Britain

W w winter visitor

V v isolated visitors – V frequently recorded, v rarely

(b) a bird that has been known to breed in the British Isles

intr. an introduced species

reintr. once extinct in Britain, but now reintroduced

esc. an escape from captivity

Thus in the example above, the Black Redstart S P w ○ occurs in Britain principally as a summer visitor and as a passage migrant in spring or autumn, while a smaller number overwinter here. It is a regularly breeding species but rare and found only in a few places. Its subspecies *aterimus* never recorded in Britain at all, is distributed in Portugal and south-central Spain.

Very rare visitors, also called Accidentals or Vagrants, are not included in the main part of this book if they have been recorded in Europe less than 20 times. But they are listed on pp. 56–8, with the countries from which they come and the parts of Europe in which they have been seen.

In the Accidentals section, a heavy *black* line indicates a new Family. Both here and for vagrants in the main section, on the right are: *above* the short line, the countries from which the birds come; and *below* it where they have been seen.

☐ **Sandhill Crane**	v.esc. ?	N. America
Grus canadensis		Ireland
☐ **Siberian Crane**	–	Asia
Grus leucogeranus		Sweden

DIVERS: *Gaviidae* 3:1 – 4:0

☐ **GREAT NORTHERN D.** W(b) ▲
Gavia immer Mostly seen along British coasts in winter plumage. A few summer on Scottish lochs.

☐ **WHITE-BILLED DIVER** V
Gavia adamsii Larger and paler in winter. Swims with pale beak pointing upwards.

☐ **BLACK-THROATED DIVER** R W ◑
Gavia arctica Winters on sea-coasts; breed on Scottish freshwater lochs. Loud wailing, laughing calls.

☐ **RED-THROATED DIVER** R p W ◑
Gavia stellata The smallest, commonest British diver: about 700 breeding pairs. Voice less deep, more musical.

GREBES: *Podicipedidae* 5:1 – 5:1

☐ **LITTLE GREBE** R w ●
Tachybaptus ruficollis Or 'Dabchick'. Most widespread British grebe, even found on small farm ponds. Trilling call.

☐ **SLAVONIAN GREBE** W r ○
Podiceps auritus About 50 British breeding pairs on Scottish lochs; wintering in sheltered bays and lakes.

☐ **BLACK-NECKED GREBE** W P s ○ ↓
Podiceps nigricollis Only some 20 British breeding pairs, on shallow lakes with cover. Gregarious in winter.

☐ **GREAT CRESTED GREBE** R w ●
Podiceps cristatus Common, conspicuous. Elaborate courtship display. Lakes, in winter also at coast. Shrill barking calls.

☐ **RED-NECKED GREBE** W ▲
Podiceps grisegena Rather thick-necked. Dark crown always down to eyes. Coasts, estuaries.

STORM PETRELS: *Hydrobatidae* 3:2 – 3:2

☐ **STORM PETREL** S p ◑
Hydrobates pelagicus Small, Martin-like seabird. Follows ships. Bat-like flight.

☐ **LEACH'S PETREL** S p ○
Oceanodroma leucorrhoa Buoyant darting, hovering, flight. Does not follow ships.

☐ **WILSON'S PETREL** v
Oceanites oceanicus Flight stronger than Storm P., more gliding. Follows ships.

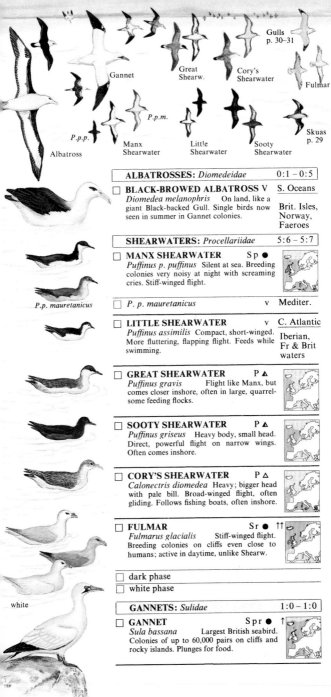

Gulls
p. 30–31

Gannet

Great
Shearw.

Cory's
Shearwater

Fulmar

P.p.m.

P.p.p.

Manx
Shearwater

Little
Shearwater

Sooty
Shearwater

Skuas
p. 29

Albatross

ALBATROSSES: *Diomedeidae*	0:1 – 0:5

☐ **BLACK-BROWED ALBATROSS** V
Diomedea melanophris On land, like a giant Black-backed Gull. Single birds now seen in summer in Gannet colonies.

S. Oceans

Brit. Isles,
Norway,
Faeroes

SHEARWATERS: *Procellariidae*	5:6 – 5:7

☐ **MANX SHEARWATER** S p ●
Puffinus p. puffinus Silent at sea. Breeding colonies very noisy at night with screaming cries. Stiff-winged flight.

P.p. mauretanicus

☐ *P. p. mauretanicus* v Mediter.

☐ **LITTLE SHEARWATER** v
Puffinus assimilis Compact, short-winged. More fluttering, flapping flight. Feeds while swimming.

C. Atlantic

Iberian,
Fr & Brit
waters

☐ **GREAT SHEARWATER** P ▲
Puffinus gravis Flight like Manx, but comes closer inshore, often in large, quarrelsome feeding flocks.

☐ **SOOTY SHEARWATER** P ▲
Puffinus griseus Heavy body, small head. Direct, powerful flight on narrow wings. Often comes inshore.

☐ **CORY'S SHEARWATER** P △
Calonectris diomedea Heavy; bigger head with pale bill. Broad-winged flight, often gliding. Follows fishing boats, often inshore.

☐ **FULMAR** S r ● ↑↑
Fulmarus glacialis Stiff-winged flight. Breeding colonies on cliffs even close to humans; active in daytime, unlike Shearw.

☐ dark phase
☐ white phase

white

GANNETS: *Sulidae*	1:0 – 1:0

☐ **GANNET** S p r ● ↑
Sula bassana Largest British seabird. Colonies of up to 60,000 pairs on cliffs and rocky islands. Plunges for food.

7

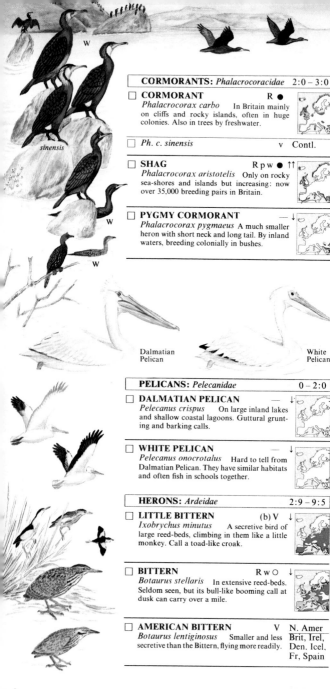

CORMORANTS: *Phalacrocoracidae*   2:0 – 3:0

☐ **CORMORANT**   R ●
Phalacrocorax carbo   In Britain mainly on cliffs and rocky islands, often in huge colonies. Also in trees by freshwater.

☐ *Ph. c. sinensis*   v Contl.

☐ **SHAG**   R p w ● ↑↑
Phalacrocorax aristotelis   Only on rocky sea-shores and islands but increasing: now over 35,000 breeding pairs in Britain.

☐ **PYGMY CORMORANT**   —
Phalacrocorax pygmaeus A much smaller heron with short neck and long tail. By inland waters, breeding colonially in bushes.

Dalmatian
Pelican

White
Pelican

PELICANS: *Pelecanidae*   0 – 2:0

☐ **DALMATIAN PELICAN**   —
Pelecanus crispus   On large inland lakes and shallow coastal lagoons. Guttural grunting and barking calls.

☐ **WHITE PELICAN**   —
Pelecanus onocrotalus   Hard to tell from Dalmatian Pelican. They have similar habitats and often fish in schools together.

HERONS: *Ardeidae*   2:9 – 9:5

☐ **LITTLE BITTERN**   (b) V
Ixobrychus minutus   A secretive bird of large reed-beds, climbing in them like a little monkey. Call a toad-like croak.

☐ **BITTERN**   R w ○
Botaurus stellaris   In extensive reed-beds. Seldom seen, but its bull-like booming call at dusk can carry over a mile.

☐ **AMERICAN BITTERN**   V   N. Amer
Botaurus lentiginosus   Smaller and less   Brit, Irel,
secretive than the Bittern, flying more readily. Den. Icel,
Fr, Spain

☐ **GREY HERON** R w ●
Ardea cinerea Ash-grey. Often seen standing motionless by streams, in meadows and wetlands. Nests colonially in trees.

☐ **PURPLE HERON** V
Ardea purpurea A more colourful, darker, smaller, elegant heron. More restricted to marshes, breeding in reed-beds.

☐ **GREAT WHITE EGRET** V ↓
Egretta alba The largest white heron. Brackish or freshwater habitats. Breeds colonially in reed-beds.

☐ **LITTLE EGRET** V
Egretta garzetta A small heron, usually hunting in shallow water. Nests near water in trees, in mixed colonies.

☐ **CATTLE EGRET** V ↑
Bulbulcus ibis Small, compact. Often with grazing cattle or horses, even in drier areas.

☐ **SQUACCO HERON** V ↓
Ardeola ralloides Very secretive, in swamps and marshes. The bulkiest-looking heron. Wings strikingly white in flight.

☐ **NIGHT HERON** V
Nycticorax nycticorax Usually seen at dusk, hunting from trees beside marshes or rivers. Colonies nest in trees.

STORKS: *Ciconiidae* 0:2 – 2:0

☐ **BLACK STORK** V ↑
Ciconia nigra A solitary, shy bird of wooded country. Feeds near water but nests only in trees of large virgin forests.

☐ **WHITE STORK** V ↓↓
Ciconia ciconia Not shy. Nests on village roofs, in S. also on trees. Feeds in wet grassland. Typical bill 'clacking'.

IBISES: *Threskiornithidae* 1:1 – 2:1

☐ **SPOONBILL** P △
Platalea leucorodia Unique bill for sifting food. Breeds in reed-beds of large freshwater marshes, in S. also on trees.

☐ **GLOSSY IBIS** V ↓
Plegadis falcinellus Appears black. Nests in reeds, rarely trees. often in heron and spoonbill colonies.

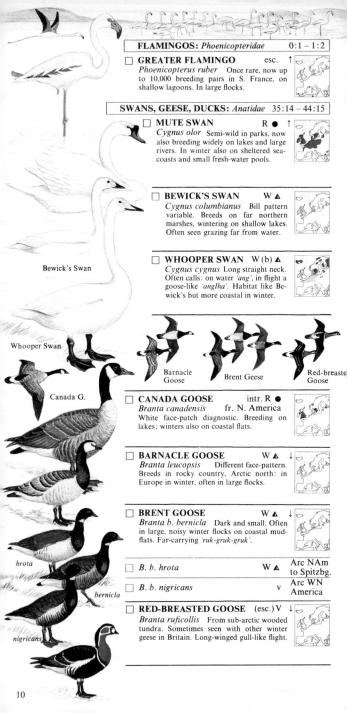

FLAMINGOS: *Phoenicopteridae* 0:1 – 1:2

☐ **GREATER FLAMINGO** esc. ↑
Phoenicopterus ruber Once rare, now up to 10,000 breeding pairs in S. France, on shallow lagoons. In large flocks.

SWANS, GEESE, DUCKS: *Anatidae* 35:14 – 44:15

☐ **MUTE SWAN** R ● ↑
Cygnus olor Semi-wild in parks, now also breeding widely on lakes and large rivers. In winter also on sheltered sea-coasts and small fresh-water pools.

☐ **BEWICK'S SWAN** W ▲
Cygnus columbianus Bill pattern variable. Breeds on far northern marshes, wintering on shallow lakes. Often seen grazing far from water.

☐ **WHOOPER SWAN** W(b) ▲
Cygnus cygnus Long straight neck. Often calls: on water *'ang'*, in flight a goose-like *'anglha'*. Habitat like Bewick's but more coastal in winter.

Bewick's Swan

Whooper Swan

Barnacle Goose

Brent Geese

Red-breasted Goose

Canada G.

☐ **CANADA GOOSE** intr. R ●
Branta canadensis fr. N. America
White face-patch diagnostic. Breeding on lakes; winters also on coastal flats.

☐ **BARNACLE GOOSE** W ▲ ↓
Branta leucopsis Different face-pattern. Breeds in rocky country, Arctic north: in Europe in winter, often in large flocks.

☐ **BRENT GOOSE** W ▲ ↓
Branta b. bernicla Dark and small. Often in large, noisy winter flocks on coastal mud-flats. Far-carrying *'ruk-gruk-gruk'*.

☐ *B. b. hrota* W ▲ Arc NAm to Spitzbg.

hrota

☐ *B. b. nigricans* v Arc WN America

bernicla

☐ **RED-BREASTED GOOSE** (esc.)V ↓
Branta ruficollis From sub-arctic wooded tundra. Sometimes seen with other winter geese in Britain. Long-winged gull-like flight.

nigricans

□ **BEAN GOOSE** W △
Anser f. fabalis More silent than other 'grey' geese.' Breeds under trees in far northern taiga. May winter far inland.

□ *A. f. rossicus* v tundra

□ **PINK-FOOTED GOOSE** W △
Anser brachyrhynchus Smaller; shorter bill, pink legs. Flight call shrill *'wink-wink'*. Not far inland in winter.

□ **WHITE-FRONTED GOOSE** W △
Anser a. albifrons White forehead. Black barrings variable. In winter often with Bean Geese on grasslands, less often fields.

□ *A. a. flavirostris* W △ W.Greenl.

□ **LESSER WHITE-FRONTED G.** V
Anser erythropus Smaller, shorter neck, bill. Wing-beats quicker, calls shriller.

Bean G.   Pink-footed G.   White-fronted G.   Egyptian G.

□ **GREYLAG GOOSE** W r ○ ↑
Anser a. anser Only British breeding 'grey' goose. On freshwater lakes and lowland moors near grassland. Calls like domestic goose.

□ *A. a. rubrirostris* (intr.) eastern

□ **SNOW GOOSE** w △
Anser caerulescens Usually with other 'grey' geese. White phase always with black wing-tips; blue with white head.

□ "Blue Goose"

□ **BAR-HEADED GOOSE** Himalaya
Anser indicus Not well established; but had bred several countries.
intr. Germany/ Sweden

□ **EGYPTIAN GOOSE** intr. R ○
Alopochen aegyptiacus fr. Africa
Exotic, long-legged Duck of goose-like habits. Well established in Britain.

□ brown phase

ossicus

fabalis

esser White-
onted Goose

rirostris

ue Goose

grey

brown

11

♀

♂

♀

♂

♀ very much like
Wigeon ♀

♂

♀ resembles other
teal ♀ ♀, brighter

♂

♂ carolinensis
♀ like ♀ c. crecca

☐ **SHELDUCK** R w ●
Tadorna tadorna Mostly near shore, rarely
far inland. Nests in burrow. Pairs or families
when breeding, large flocks in autumn.

☐ **RUDDY SHELDUCK** esc. V ↓
Tadorna ferruginea Brackish and freshwater habitats, also drier steppes. Loud, far-
carrying nasal *'ah-ong'* call.

☐ **MANDARIN DUCK** intro R ○
Aix galericulata fr. China
Nests in old tree-holes in open woods with
ponds or streams. Now 300 breeding pairs in
Britain.

☐ **WOOD DUCK** esc. (b) N. Amer.
Aix sponsa Habitat as Mandarin's. Germany
Readily uses nest-boxes. Not yet well estab-
lished here.

☐ **WIGEON** W p r ○
Anas penelope Short bill, round head.
Breeds on freshwater, winters also by coast.
Often grazes in fields like geese. Whistling
'whee-oo' calls.

☐ **AMERICAN WIGEON** V N. Amer.
Anas americana Same habitats as in most
Wigeon. Soft *'whee-whee-whee'* whistle. European
countries

☐ **GADWALL** W s R ◐
Anas strepera Floats high in water, black
rear conspicuous. Lakes with dense fringe of
vegetation, also more open waters in winter.

☐ **BAIKAL TEAL** esc. v E. Siberia
Anas formosa Possibly only escapes in in most
Europe. Drake has a clucking *'wot-wot'*. European
countries

☐ **TEAL** R p W ●
Anas c. crecca Smallest European duck,
often in tight flocks on freshwater, in winter
also near coasts, and on mountain streams.
Drake has *'crick-crick'* call.

☐ *A. c. carolinensis,* V N. Amer.
Green-winged Teal in most
European
countries

☐ **MALLARD** R w p ● ↑
Anas platyrhynchos Our commonest
duck. On all kinds of freshwater, even small
pools. In winter also near coast. Often seen in
aberrant colours – crosses with domestic
ducks.

☐ **PINTAIL** r p W ○
Anas acuta Slender body, long neck and tail. Fast flight. Feeds upside down like Mallard. Likes wide open waters.

☐ **GARGANEY** S p ◐
Anas querquedula Head pattern distinctive in both sexes. Habitats like Teal's, but not mountains and less at coast. Winters in Africa, down to the far south.

☐ **BLUE-WINGED TEAL** V N. Amer.
Anas discors Often seen in waterfowl in most collections. European countries

♀ like Garganey ♀

☐ **SHOVELER** r s p W ◐
Anas clypeata Heavy, spoon-shaped bill distinctive in both sexes. Shallow freshwater lakes and marshes, in winter also along coast.

☐ **MARBLED TEAL** —
Anas angustirostris Small, pale-looking; dark mask. Densely vegetated fresh and brackish waters. In winter, more open lakes.

☐ **RED-CRESTED POCHARD** w s △
Netta rufina Large-headed silhouette. Breeds on lakes with dense reed-beds. In winter often large flocks. Rarely saltwater.

☐ **POCHARD** r p W ○ ↑
Aythya ferina Male's black breast and rear with brown head. In winter also at coast, often in large flocks.

☐ **FERRUGINOUS DUCK** w △ ↓
Aythya nyroca White under-tail coverts. Still freshwaters with dense vegetation, also small pools, even in woods.

☐ **TUFTED DUCK** R W ●
Aythya fuligula Often with Mallards on park lakes. Breeds on open waters with reed-beds. Dives constantly.

☐ **RING-NECKED DUCK** V N. Amer.
Aythya collaris Like Tufted, but no in most crest, 'peak' headed. Neck ring only visible European close to. Bill better field-mark. countries

☐ **SCAUP** p W (b) △
Aythya marila Breeds on northern tundra. At coastal waters in winter. Like Tufted Duck with pale back. Dives well, even in rough sea.

13

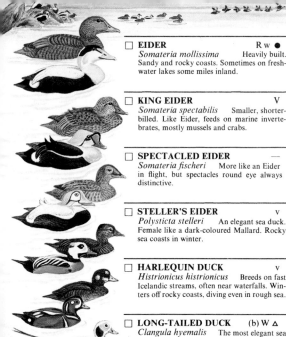

- [ ] **EIDER** R w ●
Somateria mollissima Heavily built. Sandy and rocky coasts. Sometimes on freshwater lakes some miles inland.

- [ ] **KING EIDER** V
Somateria spectabilis Smaller, shorter-billed. Like Eider, feeds on marine invertebrates, mostly mussels and crabs.

- [ ] **SPECTACLED EIDER** — Siberia
Somateria fischeri More like an Eider in flight, but spectacles round eye always distinctive. Arctic waters just N Norway

- [ ] **STELLER'S EIDER** v
Polysticta stelleri An elegant sea duck. Female like a dark-coloured Mallard. Rocky sea coasts in winter.

- [ ] **HARLEQUIN DUCK** v
Histrionicus histrionicus Breeds on fast Icelandic streams, often near waterfalls. Winters off rocky coasts, diving even in rough sea.

- [ ] **LONG-TAILED DUCK** (b) W △
Clangula hyemalis The most elegant sea duck. Drake very noisy. Breeds on both fresh and salt water. Winters along coasts.

- [ ] **COMMON SCOTER** r P W ○
Melanitta nigra Male the only wholly black duck. Breeds on tundra, winters only in coastal waters, often in large flocks.

- [ ] **VELVET SCOTER** p W △
Melanitta fusca Larger, with white wing-bar. In winter often on freshwater lakes. Forms smaller parties, with other seaducks.

- [ ] **SURF SCOTER** V N. Amer.
Melanitta perspicillata Large eider-like bill and white head-pattern. Strictly marine in winter. most N. European waters to France

- [ ] **GOLDENEYE** r p W ○
Bucephala clangula Wings make a loud, whistling, bell-like sound in flight. In winter on open fresh and coastal waters.

- [ ] **BARROW'S GOLDENEYE** v
Bucephala islandica Unlike tree-nesting goldeneye, nests in holes among rocks or walls. Winters on inshore waters.

14

☐ **GOOSANDER** r W ⦿ ↓
Mergus merganser Nests in cavities of
trees or banks, sometimes in vegetation, near
lochs and rivers. Seldom coastal in winter.

☐ **RED-BREASTED MERGANSER**
Mergus serrator R W ⦿
Ground-nesting. Mainly coastal. Uncommon
on freshwater.

☐ **SMEW** W △
Mergus albellus Small lakes in conifer
woods. Winters on lakes and estuaries. Fish-
eating, like other two sawbills above.

☐ **WHITE-HEADED DUCK** — ↓
Oxyura leucocephala Swollen blue bill,
white head. Often swims with tail cocked up.
Shallow fresh and brackish lakes.

☐ **RUDDY DUCK** intr. R ○
Oxyura jamaicensis fr. N. Amer.
Now well established in Britain: nearly 100
breeding pairs on small freshwater lakes.

OSPREY: *Pandionidae* 1:0 – 1:0

☐ **OSPREY** s P ○
Pandion haliaetus Now re-established in
Scotland. Needs large trees for nesting, and
open water for fishing.

BIRDS OF PREY: *Accipitridae* 10:4 – 27:5

☐ **EGYPTIAN VULTURE** — ↓↓
Neophron percnopterus Mountains and
lowlands. More solitary than other vultures.
Often on refuse tips with Ravens and Black
Kites. Mountain and lowland.

☐ **BLACK VULTURE** — ↓↓
Aegypius monachus Mountains and lowlands. Less gregarious than Griffon. Soars,
often at great height.

☐ **GRIFFON VULTURE** — ↓↓
Gyps fulvus Mountains. Gregarious, esp.
round carcasses. Colonial cliff-nester. Soars,
mainly in small parties.

☐ **LAMMERGEIER** — ↓↓
Gypaetus barbatus High mountains,
mainly above tree-line. In flight like a giant
falcon. Nests on rock ledges. Young much
darker.

Golden E. *A.h.heliaca* Imperial E. *A.h.adalberti*

imm.

☐ **GOLDEN EAGLE** R ◐ ↓
Aquila chrysaetos Once widespread, now restricted to high country. Beautiful soaring flight. Rather silent.

imm.

☐ **IMPERIAL EAGLE** — ↓
Aquila h. heliaca Large, plump. Buzzard-like habits. Raven-like barking call. Open lowland forests, steppes, marshes.

☐ *A. h. adalberti* — Spain

☐ **STEPPE EAGLE** —
Aquila rapax Rather stodgy-looking. Tends to stay on the ground. Flies low, seldom soars. Immatures buff-coloured.

☐ **LESSER SPOTTED EAGLE** — ↓
Aquila pomarina In wooded country with open space for hunting. Takes only small prey. Nests in trees.

☐ **SPOTTED EAGLE** —
Aquila clanga Resembles Golden Eagle, but dumpier. Open wooded country near water or marshes. Shrill dog-like barking.

← ☐ pale phase (rare) —

☐ **BONELLI'S EAGLE** — ↓
Hieraaetus fasciatus Powerful and secretive. Flight rapid. Hunts like a hawk or falcon in dry rocky country.

☐ **BOOTED EAGLE** —
Hieraaetus pennatus Open hilly country with oakwoods. Noisy with a wader-like whistling. Buoyant flight. Takes small prey.

dark ☐ dark phase

☐ **SHORT-TOED EAGLE** — ↓
Circaetus gallicus Big owl-like head, long broad wings, long tail. Often hovers. Hunts snakes and other reptiles.

pale dark

pale dark ☐ dark phase

16

☐ **WHITE-TAILED EAGLE**   V ↓
Haliaeetus albicilla   till 1916 r reintr.
Never found far from open water, salt or
fresh. Broad winged, stocky. Adult's tail white,
immature's dark.

buteo ☐   ☐   ☐   ☐

☐ **BUZZARD**   R p w ●
Buteo b. buteo   Commonest predator after
Kestrel. Seen perched on fences or posts in
open wooded country.

vulpinus ☐

vulpinus

☐ *B. b. vulpinus*   —   S. eastern

☐ **ROUGH-LEGGED BZD.**   W △
Buteo lagopus   White unbarred tail with
dark band. Black patch at angle of pale underwing. Often hovers.

dark

normal

☐ dark phase

☐ **LONG-LEGGED BUZZARD**   —
Buteo rufinus   Like Buzzard very variable
but tail always unbarred. Flight more eagle-
like. Often in quite treeless country.

black

☐ black phase

normal

☐ **RED KITE**   R ○ ↓
Milvus milvus   Elegant, long-winged;
deeply forked long tail. Open wooded country
with old broadleafed trees.

☐ **BLACK KITE**   V
Milvus migrans   Tail shorter, less forked.
Gregarious. Open wooded country, mostly
near water.

☐   ☐   ☐

☐   ☐

☐ **HONEY BUZZARD**   S p ○
Pernis apivorus   Long tail double-banded.
Small head with yellow eyes. Food mainly
wasp grubs, also very small animals and fruit.

☐ **GOSHAWK** esc. R p ○ ↓
Accipiter gentilis Shy and secretive.
Hunts by surprise from hidden forest perch.
Flight powerful, rapid, agile.

☐ *A. g. buteoides* — northern

☐ **SPARROWHAWK** R p w ●
Accipiter nisus Like a small Goshawk.
Habits similar but also in more open woods,
upland scrub, town suburbs. Calls *'kek'*,
'kew-kew'.

☐ **LEVANT SPARROWHAWK** —
Accipiter brevipes In open country,
broadleaved valleys. Voice a shrill, high-
pitched *'ke-wick-wick'*.

☐ **BLACK-SHOULDERED KITE** — ↑
Elanus caeruleus Small, pale with black
shoulders. Often on exposed perches in open
country. Hovers often.

Montagu's Harrier Hen Harrier Pallid Harrier Marsh Harrier

black phase

☐ **MONTAGU'S HARRIER** S p ○ ↓
Circus pygargus Slimmer, narrower wings
than Hen H. Voice shrill *'yick yick yick'*.

☐ black phase

☐ **HEN HARRIER** R p W ◐ ↓
Circus cyaneus White rump patch. Male
looks white with black wing-tips. Aerial
display flight. Call *'kek-kek-kek'*. Moors,
marshes, also fields.

☐ **PALLID HARRIER** v
Circus macrourus Smallest and palest
Harrier. Open plains and steppes. Female
has pale collar.

☐ **MARSH HARRIER** S R p ○ ↓↓
Circus aeruginosus Largest, with broader
wings. Hunts low over reeds, gliding and
soaring like other Harriers. Marshes, reed-
beds.

18

juv. Golden Eagle
p. 16   wingspan 210

Imperial Eagle   p. 16 wsp. 190

Steppe Eagle   wsp. 180

White-tailed Eagle   p. 17 wsp. 225

Lesser Spotted Eagle
p. 16 wsp. 150

Spotted Eagle
p. 16 wsp. 160

Rough-legged Buzzard
p. 17 wsp. 140

Buzzard
p. 17 wsp. 130

Buzzard, pale
p. 17 wsp. 130

Long-legged Buzzard
p. 17 wsp. 145

Booted Eagle, dark
p. 16 wsp. 120

Booted Eagle, pale
p. 16 wsp. 120

Bonelli's Eagle
p. 16 wsp. 170

Honey Buzzard
p. 16 wsp. 130

Honey Buzzard
p. 16 wsp. 130

Goshawk
p. 18 wsp. 110

Red Kite
p. 17 wsp. 160

Black Kite
p. 17 wsp. 150

Marsh Harrier
p. 18 wsp. 120

Osprey
p. 15 wsp. 160

Short-toed Eagle
p. 16 wsp. 180

wsp. = wingspan in cm

19

FALCONS: *Falconidae*   4:4 – 10:2

☐ **HOBBY**   S p ○ ↓
Falco subbuteo   Swift-like flight silhouette, hunting insects, small birds. Open country, wood edges.

☐ **ELEONORA'S FALCON**   v
Falco eleonorae   Sea cliffs, rocky islands. Breeds in colonies, late in season. Hunts small migrating birds over sea.

☐ dark phase

☐ **PEREGRINE**   R p w ◐ ↓
Falco p. peregrinus   Powerful, hunting birds up to crow size. Now mainly restricted to hills, breeding on cliffs. Winters mostly near water.

☐ *F. p. brookei*   —   southern

☐ **SAKER FALCON**   — ↓
Falco cherrug   Longer wings, tail. More open steppe country. Hunts larger birds, also mammals.

☐ **LANNER FALCON**   — ↓
Falco biarmicus   Smaller than Peregrine, takes smaller prey. Flight slower, tail longer. Open country, esp. near cliffs.

☐ **GYR FALCON**   v ↓
Falco rusticolus   Large, pale even in dark phase. Broad wings, long tail, slow wingbeats. Wild rough country, often near sea.

☐ white form   v

☐ **MERLIN**   R s p w ◐
Falco columbarius   Small, compact. Often imitates Mistle Thrush flight when hunting small birds. Treeless country in hills.

☐ **RED-FOOTED FALCON**   V
Falco vespertinus   Gregarious, long wings, short tail. Hunts insects, small rodents, often at sunset. Hovers like Kestrel. Open country.

☐ **KESTREL**   R s p w ●
Falco tinnunculus   Commonest raptor. Often along roads, sitting on posts or hovering. Farms, open country, also towns.

☐ **LESSER KESTREL**   v
Falco naumanni   Active, noisy; breeds colonially, often on buildings. Flight looser. But hard to tell from Kestrel.

GROUSE: Tetraonidae · · · · · · · · · · · · · 4:0 – 5:0

☐ **WILLOW GROUSE**
Lagopus l. lagopus   Dark winged form
(Red Grouse) unchanged in winter. Loud
'go-bak go-bak-bak-bak' call. Moorland.

☐ *L. l. scoticus* Red Grouse   R ● Britain
Ireland

☐ **PTARMIGAN**   R ◑ ↓
Lagopus mutus   Smaller. Wings
always white. Hoarse crackling *'ku-uk-uk,
karr-ork-kakarr'*. High stony mountains.

☐ **BLACK GROUSE**   R ◑ ↓↓
Tetrao tetrix   Flight mostly higher.
Longer tail, neck. Often glides. Wood edges,
moors, often among birch.

☐ **CAPERCAILLIE**   reintr. R ◑ ↓↓
Tetrao urogallus   fr. Scandinavia
Large conifer woodland bird. Often on
ground in summer, winter more in trees.
Noisy flapping take-off, powerful flight.

☐ **HAZELHEN**   — ↓↓
Bonasa bonasia   Hill and mountain
mixed woods with aspen, birch. Mostly in
trees. High tit-like whistle *'tsesse-tse'*.

☐ southern forms   —

TURKEY: Meleagrididae · · · · · · · · · · · · · 0 – 1:0

☐ **WILD TURKEY**   — N. Amer.
Meleagris gallopavo   Slenderer than
domestic bird. Dense woods, oak, beech.   intro.
Germany

GAME BIRDS: Phasianidae · · · · · · · · · · 7:0 – 13:0

☐ **PHEASANT**   intr. R ●
Phasianus colchicus   fr. Asia
'Ring-necked Pheasant' mostly a mix of
different subspecies bred for shooting.

☐ old English   intr. R ○

☐ melanistic   intr. R ○

☐ **REEVES'S PHEASANT**   intr. ○   Asia
Syrmaticus reevesii   Very long tail.
Fast flight. Songbird-like twittering.   intr. many
European
countries

☐ **GOLDEN PHEASANT**   intr. R ○   China
Chrysolophus pictus   Hidden in bushes,
avoids flying. Crowing *'chak-chak'*.   intr.
Britain

☐ **LADY AMHERST'S PH.**   intr. R ○   China
Chrysolophus amherstiae   Habits like
Golden, ♀ very alike. Runs fast. *'Ssu-ik-ik'*.   intr.
Britain

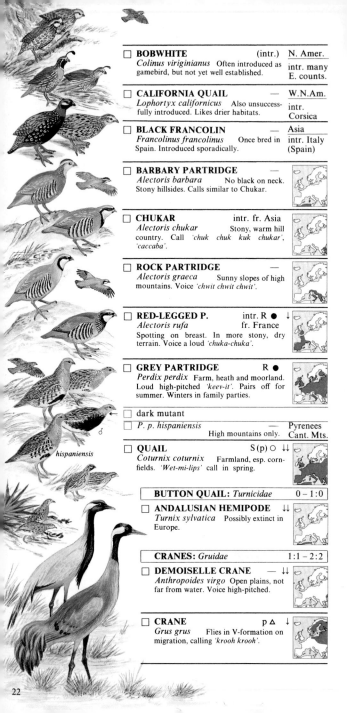

☐ **BOBWHITE** (intr.) N. Amer.
Colinus viriginianus Often introduced as gamebird, but not yet well established. intr. many E. counts.

☐ **CALIFORNIA QUAIL** — W.N.Am.
Lophortyx californicus Also unsuccessfully introduced. Likes drier habitats. intr. Corsica

☐ **BLACK FRANCOLIN** Asia
Francolinus francolinus Once bred in Spain. Introduced sporadically. intr. Italy (Spain)

☐ **BARBARY PARTRIDGE** —
Alectoris barbara No black on neck. Stony hillsides. Calls similar to Chukar.

☐ **CHUKAR** intr. fr. Asia
Alectoris chukar Stony, warm hill country. Call *'chuk chuk kuk chukar'*, *'caccaba'*.

☐ **ROCK PARTRIDGE** —
Alectoris graeca Sunny slopes of high mountains. Voice *'chwit chwit chwit'*.

☐ **RED-LEGGED P.** intr. R ● ↓
Alectoris rufa fr. France
Spotting on breast. In more stony, dry terrain. Voice a loud *'chuka-chuka'*.

☐ **GREY PARTRIDGE** R ●
Perdix perdix Farm, heath and moorland. Loud high-pitched *'keev-it'*. Pairs off for summer. Winters in family parties.

☐ dark mutant

☐ *P. p. hispaniensis* — Pyrenees
High mountains only. Cant. Mts.

☐ **QUAIL** S(p) ○ ↓↓
Coturnix coturnix Farmland, esp. cornfields. *'Wet-mi-lips'* call in spring.

| **BUTTON QUAIL:** *Turnicidae* | 0 – 1:0 |

☐ **ANDALUSIAN HEMIPODE** ↓↓
Turnix sylvatica Possibly extinct in Europe.

| **CRANES:** *Gruidae* | 1:1 – 2:2 |

☐ **DEMOISELLE CRANE** — ↓↓
Anthropoides virgo Open plains, not far from water. Voice high-pitched.

☐ **CRANE** p △ ↓
Grus grus Flies in V-formation on migration, calling *'krooh krooh'*.

hispaniensis

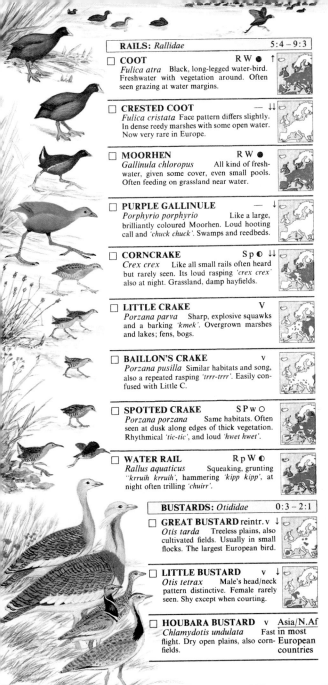

RAILS: *Rallidae* — 5:4 – 9:3

☐ **COOT**   R W ● ↑
Fulica atra   Black, long-legged water-bird. Freshwater with vegetation around. Often seen grazing at water margins.

☐ **CRESTED COOT**   — ↓↓
Fulica cristata   Face pattern differs slightly. In dense reedy marshes with some open water. Now very rare in Europe.

☐ **MOORHEN**   R W ●
Gallinula chloropus   All kind of freshwater, given some cover, even small pools. Often feeding on grassland near water.

☐ **PURPLE GALLINULE**   — ↓
Porphyrio porphyrio   Like a large, brilliantly coloured Moorhen. Loud hooting call and *'chuck chuck'*. Swamps and reedbeds.

☐ **CORNCRAKE**   Sp ◐ ↓↓
Crex crex   Like all small rails often heard but rarely seen. Its loud rasping *'crex crex'* also at night. Grassland, damp hayfields.

☐ **LITTLE CRAKE**   V
Porzana parva   Sharp, explosive squawks and a barking *'kmek'*. Overgrown marshes and lakes; fens, bogs.

☐ **BAILLON'S CRAKE**   v
Porzana pusilla   Similar habitats and song, also a repeated rasping *'trrr-trrr'*. Easily confused with Little C.

☐ **SPOTTED CRAKE**   S P w ◐
Porzana porzana   Same habitats. Often seen at dusk along edges of thick vegetation. Rhythmical *'tic-tic'*, and loud *'hwet hwet'*.

☐ **WATER RAIL**   R p W ◐
Rallus aquaticus   Squeaking, grunting *"krruih krruih"*, hammering *'kipp kipp'*, at night often trilling *'chuirr'*.

BUSTARDS: *Otididae* — 0:3 – 2:1

☐ **GREAT BUSTARD** reintr. v ↓
Otis tarda   Treeless plains, also cultivated fields. Usually in small flocks. The largest European bird.

☐ **LITTLE BUSTARD**   v ↓
Otis tetrax   Male's head/neck pattern distinctive. Female rarely seen. Shy except when courting.

☐ **HOUBARA BUSTARD**   v   Asia/N.Af
Chlamydotis undulata   Fast in most flight. Dry open plains, also corn- European fields.   countries

PLOVERS: *Charadriidae*   7:8 – 8:8

☐ **LAPWING**   R S P W ●
Vanellus vanellus   Wet grasslands, moors, fields; in winter also coastal flats. Often in large flocks. Flapping flight, shrill *'pee-wit'*.

☐ **SOCIABLE PLOVER**   v   Asia
Chettusia gregaria   Truly a sociable: seen   in most
in Britain with Lapwings. Short whistle *'etch*   European
etch etch'.   countries

☐ **SPUR-WINGED PLOVER**   —
Hoplopterus spinosus   Strikingly black-and-white. Noisy, with high-pitched *'zikoeek'*. Open country and salt flats.

☐ **KILLDEER**   V   N. Amer.
Charadrius vociferus   Habitat more like   Brit. Irel.
Lapwing than other plovers. Call *'kill-dee'*.   Fr. Swiss.
  Faer. Icel.

☐ **RINGED PLOVER**   R P W ●
Charadrius hiaticula   Sand and shingle shores. Also inland mudflats in winter.

☐ *Ch. h. tundrae*   —   northern

☐ **LITTLE RINGED PLOVER**   S ○ ↓
Charadrius dubius   Shingle by rivers and reservoirs, also gravel pits. Not gregarious.

☐ **KENTISH PLOVER**   P (b) △
Charadrius alexandrinus   Pale. Rather long-legged. No breastband, only patches. Sandy or muddy sea-shores.

☐ **DOTTEREL**   S P ○
Eudromias morinellus   Bare stony mountains. On migrations also uplands, lowland fields, coastal marshes. Pallid in winter.

☐ **GREY PLOVER**   P W ▲
Pluvialis squatarola   Thick-billed, hunched look. Wades freely. Mostly small parties on mudflats, sandy beaches.

☐ **GOLDEN PLOVER**   p w △
Pluvialis apricaria   Aerial display in spring with mournful trilling song. Moors, marshes. In winter often large flocks on farms or muddy shores.

☐ southern   R P W ●

☐ **LESSER GOLDEN PLOVER**   V   NE Asia
Pluvialis dominica   Smaller; longer bill,   N. Amer.
legs. Underwing buff-grey.   in most
  Eur. con.

□ **TURNSTONE** p w ▲
Arenaria interpres   Harlequin pattern.
Rocky and weedy shores and mudflats. In
flight twittering *'kititibit'*.

□ **SNIPE** R p W ● ↓
Gallinago gallinago   Very long bill. When
flushed, zigzag flight and harsh *'creech'*. Goat-

□ melanistic phase   mostly Irel.

melanistic

□ **GREAT SNIPE** V
Gallinago media   Bulkier, bill shorter,
sides more barred. Flight straight. More in
dry grass and heather.

□ **JACK SNIPE** p w ▲
Lymnocryptes minimus   Small, short-
billed, escape flight silent. Stays hidden till
almost trodden on. Marshes with cover.

□ **LONG-BILLED DOWITCHER** V   NE Asia
Limnodromus scolopaceus   Like Green-   N. Amer.
shank with long bill and short legs. Fresh-   in most
water mudflats.   Eur. con.

W

□ **WOODCOCK** R p W ● ↓
Scolopax rusticola   Solitary woodland
wader, secretive. Owl-like flight with drooping
bill. Active at dawn and dusk.

□ **CURLEW** R s p W ● ↓
Numenius arquata   Wary. Loud *'coour-
lee'*, alarm a fast *'kvi-kvi-kvi'*. Heaths
and farmland, winters also on mudflats
and coast.

□ **SLENDER-BILLED CURLEW** —
Numenius tenuirostris   Breast and flanks
spotted. Pure white rump in flight. Call shorter
than Curlew's. Alarm *'kew-ee'*. Mainly coastal.

□ **WHIMBREL** s P w ○ ↓
Numenius phaeopus   Head pattern, shorter
bill. Twittering whistle *'ti-ti-ti-ti'*. Winters on
coasts. *c.* 200 British breeding pairs on moors.

W

□ **BAR-TAILED GODWIT** p w ▲
Limosa lapponica   Upturned bill, shortish
legs, no white in wings. Quick loud *'kirrik
kirrik'* in flight. Mudflats, sandy shores.

□ **BLACK-TAILED GWT.** s P W ○
Limosa limosa   Barred flanks in summer,
very pale in winter. White wing-bar in flight
with *'weeka-weeka-weeka'* call.

□ *L. l. islandica*   v   Iceland

islandica

☐ **SPOTTED REDSHANK**   P w ▲
Tringa erythropus   Darkest summer wader, winter palest. Wades deeply, often swimming. Loud *'tchu-eet'*.

☐ **REDSHANK**   R P W ●
Tringa totanus   Bright red legs. Restless, noisy. Fast erratic flight. *'Tlu-leu-leu'* call. Wet meadows. Coastal marshes in winter.

☐ **LESSER YELLOWLEGS**   V   N. Amer.
Tringa flavipes   Spindly yellow legs.   most W.
Habits like Wood Sandpiper.   European countries

☐ **GREATER YELLOWLEGS**   v   N. Amer.
Tringa melanoleuca   Like Greenshank   Brit. Irel.
with bright yellow legs. Grey back in flight.   Iceland Sweden

☐ **GREENSHANK**   s P w ○
Tringa nebularia   Pale, white-faced. Strong lightly upturned bill. Clear *'teu-teu-teu'* in flight. Bare moors, open pine forests.

☐ **MARSH SANDPIPER**   V
Tringa stagnatilis   In winter like miniature, slender Greenshank with needle-bill. Active, graceful. Freshwater margins.

☐ **WOOD SANDPIPER**   s P ○
Tringa glareola   Pale underwings, spotted upperparts. *'Chiff-iff-iff'* in flight. Winters mainly on fresh water.

☐ **GREEN SANDPIPER**   P w (b) ▵
Tringa ochropus   Darker, less spotted, shorter greenish legs. Snipe-like flight. Ringing *'weet tweet-tweet'*. Mostly fresh water.

☐ **SOLITARY SANDPIPER**   v   N. Amer.
Tringa solitaria   Like small, brownish   Brit., Irl.,
Green Sandpiper. Thin *'pzit'*. Piping *'peet-   Fr., Ger.,
weet'*.   Iceland

☐ **SPOTTED SANDPIPER**   (b) V   N. Amer.
Actitis macularia   Hard to tell from   Brit., Irl.,
Common in winter. Sharp *'peet-weet'*.   Belgium, Germany

☐ **COMMON SANDPIPER**   S p w ●
Actitis hypoleucos   Short legs, long rear (often wags). Often on rocky streams where no other waders. Winters on lakes, estuaries. *'Tsee wee wee'*.

☐ **TEREK SANDPIPER**   v
Xenus cinereus   Like Common, with longer bill, short yellow-orange legs. Mudflats.

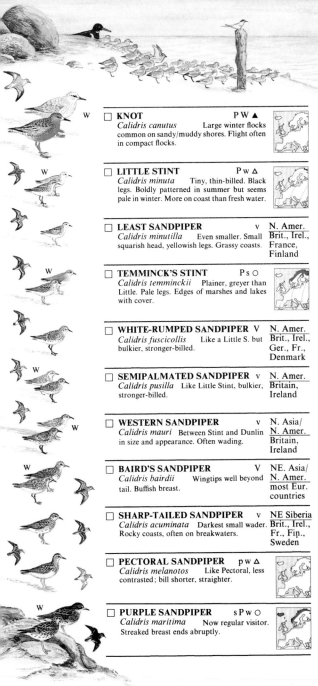

□ **KNOT** P W ▲
Calidris canutus Large winter flocks
common on sandy/muddy shores. Flight often
in compact flocks.

□ **LITTLE STINT** P w △
Calidris minuta Tiny, thin-billed. Black
legs. Boldly patterned in summer but seems
pale in winter. More on coast than fresh water.

□ **LEAST SANDPIPER** v N. Amer.
Calidris minutilla Even smaller. Small Brit., Irel.,
squarish head, yellowish legs. Grassy coasts. France,
Finland

□ **TEMMINCK'S STINT** P s ○
Calidris temminckii Plainer, greyer than
Little. Pale legs. Edges of marshes and lakes
with cover.

□ **WHITE-RUMPED SANDPIPER** V N. Amer.
Calidris fuscicollis Like a Little S. but Brit., Irel.,
bulkier, stronger-billed. Ger., Fr.,
Denmark

□ **SEMIPALMATED SANDPIPER** v N. Amer.
Calidris pusilla Like Little Stint, bulkier, Britain,
stronger-billed. Ireland

□ **WESTERN SANDPIPER** v N. Asia/
Calidris mauri Between Stint and Dunlin N. Amer.
in size and appearance. Often wading. Britain,
Ireland

□ **BAIRD'S SANDPIPER** V NE. Asia/
Calidris bairdii Wingtips well beyond N. Amer.
tail. Buffish breast. most Eur.
countries

□ **SHARP-TAILED SANDPIPER** v NE Siberia
Calidris acuminata Darkest small wader. Brit., Irel.,
Rocky coasts, often on breakwaters. Fr., Fin.,
Sweden

□ **PECTORAL SANDPIPER** p w △
Calidris melanotos Like Pectoral, less
contrasted; bill shorter, straighter.

□ **PURPLE SANDPIPER** s P w ○
Calidris maritima Now regular visitor.
Streaked breast ends abruptly.

□ **DUNLIN** P W ▲
Calidris a. alpina Commonest small wader with hunched look, slightly decurved bill.

□ *C. a. schinzii* r s P W ◐ NE Grnl.
□ *C. a. arctica* p w △ SE Grnl.

□ **CURLEW SANDPIPER** s P △
Calidris ferruginea More upright. Longer legs, neck. Thinner decurved bill. White rump in flight.

□ **SANDERLING** S P W △
Calidris alba Seems white with black shoulder. Runs up and down beach with surf-line, almost as if on wheels.

□ **STILT SANDPIPER** v N. Amer.
Micropalama himantopus Like a Curlew Brit., Irel., Sandpiper but more elegant. Germany

□ **BUFF-BREASTED SANDPIPER** V NW. Am.
Tryngites subruficollis Recalls a young most Eur. Ruff with smaller head and bill. Not shy. countries

□ **BROAD-BILLED SANDPIPER** v
Limicola falcinellus Less active, solitary, secretive. Long-billed, snipe-like. Mostly vegetated inland mudflats.

□ **UPLAND SANDPIPER** v N. Amer.
Bartramia longicauda Short, thin bill. most Eur. countries

□ **RUFF** s P w ◐
Philomachus pugnax Breeds on freshwater marshes with spectacular courtship. In winter also on salt water, resembling a Redshank.

PHALAROPES: *Phalaropodidae* 2:1 – 2:1

□ **RED-NECKED PH.** s p ○
Phalaropus lobatus Pecks from side to side in the water of shallow pools, often spinning round. Winters at sea.

□ **GREY PHALAROPE** P w △
Phalaropus fulicarius Slightly larger; bill stouter. Less active. A seabird, rare inland.

□ **WILSON'S PHALAROPE** V N. Amer.
Phalaropus tricolor Long needle bill. Brit., Irel., Ice, Ger, Bel

OYSTERCATCHERS: *Haematopodidae*   1:0 – 1:0

☐ **OYSTERCATCHER**   R s p W ●
Haematopus ostralegus   Large gregarious, noisy. Loud *'peek-a-peek'*. Open shores. Also nests inland far from water.

STILTS: *Recurvirostridae*   2:0 – 2:0

☐ **AVOCET**   S r p ○
Recurvirostra avosetta   Parties on shallow brackish lagoons. Swimming, often up-ends like duck. Melodious *'kloo-iet'*.

☐ **BLACK-WINGED STILT**   (b) V
Himantopus himantopus   Long legs show in flight. Often wades in deep water. Shrill *'kik-kik-kik'*. Brackish and salt water.

THICK-KNEES: *Burhinidae*   1:0 – 1:1

☐ **STONE CURLEW**   S ○   ↓
Burhinus oedicnemus   Wailing *'coor-lee'* heard at night. Open dry stony country, heath and farmland.

PRATINCOLES: *Glareolidae*   0:3 – 2:1

☐ **BLACK-WINGED PRATINCOLE** v
Glareola nordmanni   Habits and habitat as Collared's, but rarer than Collared, darker, wings not white-edged.

☐ **COLLARED PRATINCOLE**   V
Glareola pratincola   Tern-like flight, hawking insects. Chattering *'kirik kirik'*. Dry mud flats.

☐ **CREAM-COLOURED COURSER** v   SW. Asia/
Cursorius cursor   Runs, flies fast. Dunes   Africa
and fields.   widely

SKUAS: *Stercorariidae*   4:0 – 4:0

☐ **GREAT SKUA**   S p ◑
Stercorarius skua   Seabird breeding on moors. White wing patches.

☐ **POMARINE SKUA**   P △
Stercorarius pomarinus   Pointed wings. Central tail feathers blunt, twisted. Heavy flight.

☐ dark phase

☐ **ARCTIC SKUA**   S p ◑
Stercorarius parasiticus   More graceful flight, falcon-like. Tail feathers pointed.

☐ dark phase

☐ **LONG-TAILED SKUA**   P △
Stercorarius longicaudus   Smaller, slimmer. Long flexible central tail feathers.

GULLS: Laridae	11:8 – 17:6

☐ **IVORY GULL** v
Pagophila eburnea Pure white, pigeon-like. Short legs. Tern-like flight. Seldom settles on water. Young uniquely spotted.

☐ **ICELAND GULL** W △
Larus glaucoides Herring Gull size, slimmer, rounder-headed, smaller-billed, shriller voice. Long narrow wings.

☐ **GLAUCOUS GULL** r W ○
Larus hyperboreus Heavy bill, angular head, fierce-looking. Shorter broader wings.

☐ **Glaucous x Herring Gull** occ. where
hybrid Larger gulls hybridise easily: in both breed
Iceland nearly half all pairs are Glaucous/ together
Herring. Their offspring seen in Britain in winter.

☐ **HERRING GULL** R W ● ↑↑
Larus argentatus Commonest, most widespread gull. Often large nesting colonies, mostly on coast, some inland.

☐ yellow-legged form occ. rare but regular

☐ **WHITE-HEADED GULL** — ↑↑
Larus cachinnans Like Herring Gull but legs always yellow, mantle slightly darker, head unstreaked in winter.

graellsii

☐ **LESSER BLACK-BACK** S r ●
Larus fuscus graellsii Mantle dark grey in Britain, black Scandinavia. Often breeds inland.

☐ *L. f. fuscus* P w ▲ Northern Eastern

fuscus

☐ **GREAT BLACK-BACK** R W ●
Larus marinus More solitary than Lesser, heavier flight. Predatory, piratic. Breeds on rocky islands, seldom inland.

☐ **COMMON GULL** R p W ●
Larus canus Not most common. Smaller, dark-eyed, smaller bill, rounder head. Breeds far inland on moors.

☐ **RING-BILLED GULL** v N. Amer.
Larus delawarensis Like a large Common. Stouter bill with dark tip. Pale eyes. Brit., Irel. Germany, Netherl.

30

☐ AUDOUIN'S GULL —
Larus audouinii More buoyant flight than Herring G. Dark eyes, red bill. On rocky islands and high cliffs.

☐ SLENDER-BILLED GULL v
Larus genei Larger than Black-headed, longer tail, paler and more 'long-faced' look. Wing pattern similar.

☐ MEDITERRANEAN GULL s P w ○
Larus melanocephalus Highly contrasted, no black in wing. Sometimes in colonies of Black-headed Gull and forming mixed pairs.

☐ BLACK-HEADED GULL R s p W ● ↑
Larus ridibundus Very widespread. The common town gull in winter. Breeds on coast, also large inland colonies esp. in north.

☐ LAUGHING GULL v
Larus atricilla Differs from Black-headed in black wingtip with white trailing edge.

N. Amer. Britain, France, Sweden

☐ BONAPARTE'S GULL v
Larus philadelphia Smaller than Black-headed, rounder wings, black bill.

N. Amer.

Britain

☐ LITTLE GULL P w (b) ▲
Larus minutus Small. Tern-like flight showing dark rounded underwing. Estuaries and inland lakes.

☐ GREAT BLACK-HEADED GULL v
Larus ichthyaetus Almost big as Great Blackback with dark mask and crown in winter. Graceful flight. Mainly coastal in winter.

Caspian, WC. Asia in most European countries

☐ SABINE'S GULL P w ▲
Larus sabini Graceful offshore seagull, seen rarely on coast or lagoons. Tern-like habits.

☐ KITTIWAKE R S p w ●
Rissa tridactyla Small head, short black legs. Breeding colonies on cliff ledges, sometimes port buildings. Winters mainly far at sea.

☐ ROSS'S GULL v
Rhodostethia rosea Small, dove-like, pointed wings, wedge tail, agile flight.

NE. Sib. arc. Amer.
N. Euro. waters

☐ **BLACK TERN**   s p (b) △ ↓
Chlidonias niger Commonest small broad-winged 'marsh' tern. All grey above. Black spot on side of breast in winter.

☐ **WHITE-WINGED TERN**   V
Chlidonias leucopterus Stockier, slower wing-beats. In summer black underwing covers.

☐ **WHISKERED TERN**   V
Chlidonias hybridus Looks more like Common than a 'marsh' tern. More forked tail. But actions like Black Tern.

☐ **GULL-BILLED TERN**   V ↓
Gelochelidon nilotica Stocky build. Short stout bill, long legs. Gull-like flight. Laughing throaty *'qua-huak'*. Sandy shores, also inland.

☐ **SANDWICH TERN**   S P ●
Sterna sandvicensis Similar but longer bill, shorter legs, slender build. Strong flight. Loud shrill *'kir-rik'*. Coastal, also inland.

☐ **COMMON TERN**   S P ●
Sterna hirundo Long red bill with black tip. Whiter breast than Arctic, otherwise similar. Coastal, also inland.

☐ **ARCTIC TERN**   S p ●
Sterna paradisaea Shorter, all-red bill. Tail longer, legs very short. Coastal, often breeding with Common. Not inland.

☐ **ROSEATE TERN**   S p ◐
Sterna dougallii Palest, longest-tailed of 3 similar terns. All-black bill, longer legs. Marine, nests mainly on islets.

☐ **SOOTY TERN**   v   Tropics
Sterna fuscata Oceanic, rarely near coast. most E. countries

☐ **LITTLE TERN**   S P ◐
Sterna albifrons Smallest 'sea tern'. Often hovers, dives. Less gregarious. Harsh *'kree-ik'*. Sandy coasts, seldom inland.

☐ **LESSER CRESTED TERN**   —   Afr.-Asian
Sterna bengalensis Like Sandwich T.   Australia with orange bill, white forehead.   most S. E. countries

☐ **CASPIAN TERN**   V
Sterna caspia Very large, stout bill. In flight more gull-like, with darkish primaries, forked tail.

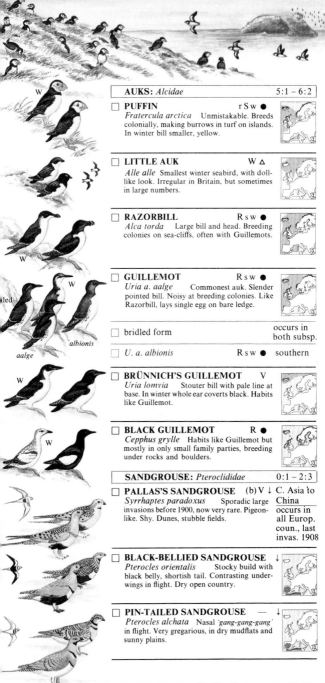

| **AUKS:** *Alcidae* | 5:1 – 6:2 |

☐ **PUFFIN** r S w ●
Fratercula arctica Unmistakable. Breeds colonially, making burrows in turf on islands. In winter bill smaller, yellow.

☐ **LITTLE AUK** W △
Alle alle Smallest winter seabird, with doll-like look. Irregular in Britain, but sometimes in large numbers.

☐ **RAZORBILL** R s w ●
Alca torda Large bill and head. Breeding colonies on sea-cliffs, often with Guillemots.

☐ **GUILLEMOT** R s w ●
Uria a. aalge Commonest auk. Slender pointed bill. Noisy at breeding colonies. Like Razorbill, lays single egg on bare ledge.

☐ bridled form
occurs in both subsp.

☐ *U. a. albionis* R s w southern

☐ **BRÜNNICH'S GUILLEMOT** V
Uria lomvia Stouter bill with pale line at base. In winter whole ear coverts black. Habits like Guillemot.

☐ **BLACK GUILLEMOT** R ●
Cepphus grylle Habits like Guillemot but mostly in only small family parties, breeding under rocks and boulders.

| **SANDGROUSE:** *Pteroclididae* | 0:1 – 2:3 |

☐ **PALLAS'S SANDGROUSE** (b) V ↓ C. Asia to China
Syrrhaptes paradoxus Sporadic large invasions before 1900, now very rare. Pigeon-like. Shy. Dunes, stubble fields.
occurs in all Europ. coun., last invas. 1908

☐ **BLACK-BELLIED SANDGROUSE** ↓
Pterocles orientalis Stocky build with black belly, shortish tail. Contrasting under-wings in flight. Dry open country.

☐ **PIN-TAILED SANDGROUSE** — ↓
Pterocles alchata Nasal *'gang-gang-gang'* in flight. Very gregarious, in dry mudflats and sunny plains.

33

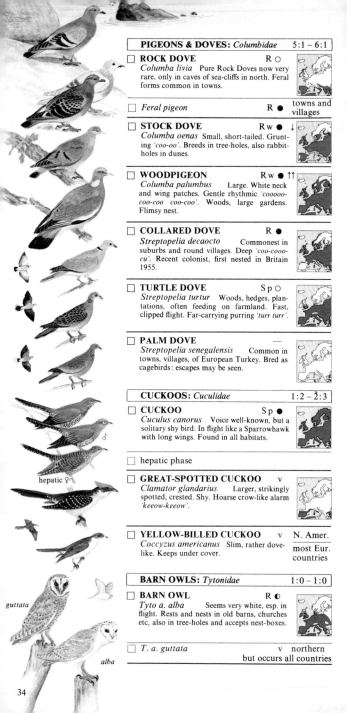

PIGEONS & DOVES: *Columbidae*   5:1 – 6:1

☐ **ROCK DOVE**   R ○
Columba livia   Pure Rock Doves now very rare, only in caves of sea-cliffs in north. Feral forms common in towns.

☐ *Feral pigeon*   R ●   towns and villages

☐ **STOCK DOVE**   R w ●   ↓
Columba oenas   Small, short-tailed. Grunting *'coo-oo'*. Breeds in tree-holes, also rabbit-holes in dunes.

☐ **WOODPIGEON**   R w ●   ↑↑
Columba palumbus   Large. White neck and wing patches. Gentle rhythmic *'cooooo-coo-coo coo-coo'*. Woods, large gardens. Flimsy nest.

☐ **COLLARED DOVE**   R ●
Streptopelia decaocto   Commonest in suburbs and round villages. Deep *'coo-cooo-cu'*. Recent colonist, first nested in Britain 1955.

☐ **TURTLE DOVE**   S p ○
Streptopelia turtur   Woods, hedges, plantations, often feeding on farmland. Fast, clipped flight. Far-carrying purring *'turr turr'*.

☐ **PALM DOVE**
Streptopelia senegalensis   Common in towns, villages, of European Turkey. Bred as cagebirds: escapes may be seen.

CUCKOOS: *Cuculidae*   1:2 – 2:3

☐ **CUCKOO**   S p ●
Cuculus canorus   Voice well-known, but a solitary shy bird. In flight like a Sparrowhawk with long wings. Found in all habitats.

☐ hepatic phase

☐ **GREAT-SPOTTED CUCKOO**   v
Clamator glandarius   Larger, strikingly spotted, crested. Shy. Hoarse crow-like alarm *'keeow-keeow'*.

☐ **YELLOW-BILLED CUCKOO**   v   N. Amer.
Coccyzus americanus   Slim, rather dove-like. Keeps under cover.   most Eur. countries

BARN OWLS: *Tytonidae*   1:0 – 1:0

☐ **BARN OWL**   R ○
Tyto a. alba   Seems very white, esp. in flight. Rests and nests in old barns, churches etc, also in tree-holes and accepts nest-boxes.

☐ *T. a. guttata*   v   northern but occurs all countries

OWLS: Strigidae 5:3 – 12:1

☐ **EAGLE OWL** —
Bubo bubo Largest European nocturnal bird. Wild forests, gorges and mountains. Deep *'ooh-hu'*.

☐ **SCOPS OWL** V
Otus scops Nocturnal. Repeated *'poo'* resembles Bell Toad. Woods, parks, often buildings. Roosts by day against trunk under cover.

☐ **SNOWY OWL** w(b) △
Nyctea scandiaca Very large. Powerful flight, active by day, often seen on ground. Has bred in Britain but now only ♀♀ resident.

☐ **HAWK OWL** v
Surnia ulula Active by day. Perches freely in the open. Dashing hawk-like flight. Long tail. Chattering *'ki-kikiki'*.

☐ **PYGMY OWL** —
Glaucidium passerinum Smallest European owl. Often active by day. Flicks tail. Conifer forests, esp. in mountains.

☐ **LITTLE OWL** intr. R ●
Athene noctua Often seen by day. Bobs about on perch. Farmland, open country with trees. Loud *'kewf kewf'*.

☐ **TAWNY OWL** R ●
Strix aluco *'Kee-wick'* and long hoots *'hoo-oo-oo-ooo ou'*. Woods, larger parks.

☐ grey phase

☐ **URAL OWL** —
Strix uralensis Longer-tailed, much larger. Barking *'hau hauu'*. Conifer woods.

☐ **GREAT GREY OWL** — ↑
Strix nebulosa Very large. Seems bigheaded. Deep hooting. Diurnal. Conifer forests.

☐ **SHORT-EARED OWL** R s p W ◐
Asio flammeus Diurnal. Open moors, marshes, dunes. Mainly ground-nesting.

☐ **LONG-EARED OWL** R p w ◐
Asio otus Nocturnal. Woods. In winter gregarious, and also more open country. Tree-nesting.

☐ **TENGMALM'S OWL** v
Aegolius funereus Nocturnal. Big-head. Conifers in hilly country. Hoopoe-like song.

grey

NIGHTJARS: *Caprimulgidae*   1:2 – 2:2

☐ **NIGHTJAR**   Sp ◑ ↑
Caprimulgus europaeus More often heard than seen; rising and falling *churr*, just after sunset.

☐ **RED-NECKED NIGHTJAR**   —
Caprimulgus ruficollis Best distinguished by its different song *'kutuk kutuk kutuk'*. Also in open country.

SWIFTS: *Apodidae*   1:5 – 4:3

☐ **SWIFT**   Sp ●
Apus apus The noisy, fast-flying bird of towns and larger villages. Nests in buildings, often in small holes.

☐ **PALLID SWIFT**   V
Apus pallidus Paler, deeper wingbeats. Some contrast in underwings. Arrives long before Swift. Also on cliffs.

☐ **ALPINE SWIFT**   V
Apus melba White underparts, dark breast-band. Kestrel-like trilling call. Large buildings, cliffs, mountains.

☐ **WHITE-RUMPED SWIFT**   —
Apus caffer Recently found breeding in Red-rumped Swallow (p. 40) colonies. Twitters there, otherwise mainly silent.

PARROTS: *Psittacidae*   1:0 – 1:0

☐ **RING-NECKED PARAKEET**
Psittacula krameri   intr. R ○ fr. India
Colonies established in Europe only recently. Sometimes noisy.

KINGFISHERS: *Alcedinidae*   1:1 – 1:3

☐ **KINGFISHER**   R ● ↓
Alcedo atthis Mostly seen flying low and fast along a stream, but also ponds, lakes. In winter also on coast.

BEE-EATERS: *Meropidae*   1:1 – 1:1

☐ **BEE-EATER**   (b) V
Merops apiaster Digs nest-holes in sandy banks like Kingfisher, but colonially. In flight a liquid *'pruup pruup'*.

ROLLERS: *Coraciidae*   0:1 – 1:0

☐ **ROLLER**   V
Coracias garrulus Flies like Jackdaw: straight ahead with some gliding. Open country. Harsh crow-like *'krrrak krak-ak'*.

HOOPOES: *Upupidae*   1:0 – 1:0

☐ **HOOPOE**   P (b) △
Upupa epops Monotonous *'hoop hoop hoop'* call in spring. Open wooded farmland, often near livestock.

WOODPECKERS: *Picidae* 4:1 →10:1

☐ **GREEN WOODPECKER** R ●
Picus v. viridis Often on ground in open broad-leaved country. Bright yellow rump in flight. Rarely drums. Call a ringing laugh.

sharpei

☐ *P. v. sharpei* — Iberia

☐ **GREY-HEADED W.**
Picus canus Prefers hilly country, avoids coniferous woods. Drums in spring. Call more musical with melancholy falling off.

☐ **BLACK WOODPECKER**
Dryocopus martius Far-carrying fluty *'klewk'*. Undulating, heavy flight. Mixed and conifer woods, often beech.

☐ **GREAT SPOTTED W.** R p w ●
Dendrocopos major Commonest woodpecker. Drums often. Sharp *'tchik'* call. Parks and woods, both deciduous and conifer.

☐ **SYRIAN WOODPECKER**
Dendrocopos syriacus Like Great Spotted with no black neck bar. Habits similar but more often in open country and near humans.

☐ **MIDDLE-SPOTTED W.** --- ↓
Dendrocopos medius Rarely drums. Repeated *'gik gik gik'* and a wailing *'weait weait'*. Oakwoods, not conifers.

☐ **WHITE-BACKED W.** ↓
Dendrocopos l. leucotos Larger but slenderer. Dense conifer hillsides. Long drumming, softer voice. Shy, difficult to observe.

☐ *D. l. lilfordi* SE. Eur. Pyrenees

☐ **LESSER SPOTTED W.** R ● ↓
Dendrocopos minor Very small. Kestrel-like *'kew-kew-kew-kew'*. Often drums. Open woodlands, parks, large gardens, orchards.

lilfordi

☐ **THREE-TOED WOODPECKER** —
Picoides t. tridactylus No red. Conifer mountain forests with Birch. Rarely drums. Slow *'kek-kek-kek'* seldom heard.

☐ *P. t. alpinus* — Alps and SE. Eur.

☐ **WRYNECK** s P ○
Jynx torquilla A 'woodpecker' with a warbler's habits. Often on ground searching for ants. Open woods and orchards.

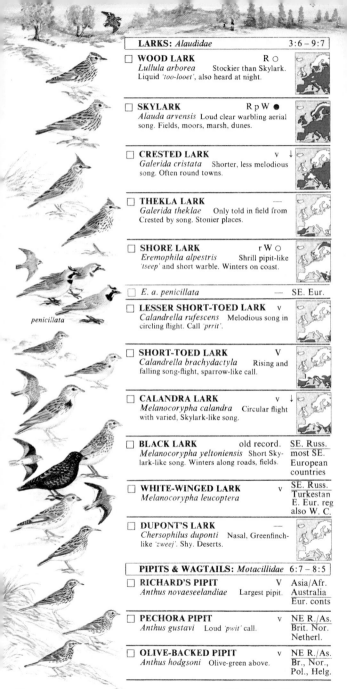

LARKS: *Alaudidae* — 3:6 – 9:7

☐ **WOOD LARK** — R ○
Lullula arborea   Stockier than Skylark.
Liquid *'too-looet'*, also heard at night.

☐ **SKYLARK** — R p W ●
Alauda arvensis   Loud clear warbling aerial
song. Fields, moors, marsh, dunes.

☐ **CRESTED LARK** — v ↓
Galerida cristata   Shorter, less melodious
song. Often round towns.

☐ **THEKLA LARK**
Galerida theklae   Only told in field from
Crested by song. Stonier places.

☐ **SHORE LARK** — r W ○
Eremophila alpestris   Shrill pipit-like
'tseep' and short warble. Winters on coast.

☐ *E. a. penicillata* — — SE. Eur.

☐ **LESSER SHORT-TOED LARK** — v
Calandrella rufescens   Melodious song in
circling flight. Call *'prrit'*.

☐ **SHORT-TOED LARK** — V
Calandrella brachydactyla   Rising and
falling song-flight, sparrow-like call.

☐ **CALANDRA LARK** — v ↓
Melanocorypha calandra   Circular flight
with varied, Skylark-like song.

☐ **BLACK LARK** — old record. SE. Russ.
Melanocorypha yeltoniensis   Short Sky-   most SE.
lark-like song. Winters along roads, fields.   European
                                               countries

☐ **WHITE-WINGED LARK** — v   SE. Russ.
Melanocorypha leucoptera   Turkestan
                                  E. Eur. reg
                                  also W. C.

☐ **DUPONT'S LARK** — —
Chersophilus duponti   Nasal, Greenfinch-
like *'zweej'*. Shy. Deserts.

PIPITS & WAGTAILS: *Motacillidae* — 6:7 – 8:5

☐ **RICHARD'S PIPIT** — V   Asia/Afr.
Anthus novaeseelandiae   Largest pipit.   Australia
                                            Eur. conts

☐ **PECHORA PIPIT** — v   NE R./As.
Anthus gustavi   Loud *'pwit'* call.   Brit. Nor.
                                         Netherl.

☐ **OLIVE-BACKED PIPIT** — v   NE R./As.
Anthus hodgsoni   Olive-green above.   Br., Nor.,
                                         Pol., Helg.

penicillata

☐ **TREE PIPIT** Sp ●
Anthus trivialis Harsh *'teez'*; repeated *'sip'* alarm; parachuting song-flight with Canary-like *'seea seea seea'*.

☐ **MEADOW PIPIT** S r P W ●
Anthus pratensis Soft *'eest eest'*; *'tissip'* alarm; parachute drop ends with whistling trill. Open country and bogs.

☐ **RED-THROATED PIPIT** v
Anthus cervinus Song less melodious than Meadow Pipit, and a hissing call. Marshes and wet fields, often near coast.

☐ **TAWNY PIPIT** v
Anthus campestris Uniformly greyish. Long, slender, wagtail-like – also in habits, voice. Song-flight *'kirlew'*.

☐ **WATER PIPIT, see also p. 57** W △
1 *Anthus sp. spinoletta* Both mountain and coastal populations. Winters in plain.

☐ 2 *A. sp. petrosus*, Rock Pipit R ● Eur. coasts

☐ 3 *A. sp. littoralis* v Den. Swe.

☐ **YELLOW WAGTAIL** (b) V
1 *Motacilla fl. flava* Vary variable. Moorland, damp heaths, pastures, often with livestock. Never far from water.

☐ 2 *M. fl. flavissima* S ● Britain

☐ 3 *M. fl. beema* v Russia

☐ 4 *M. fl. thunbergi* v N. Scand.

☐ 5 *M. fl. feldegg* — Balkans

☐ 6 *M. fl. cinereocapilla* v Italy

☐ 7 *M. fl. iberiae* — Iberia S. France

☐ **GREY WAGTAIL** R s ●
Motacilla cinerea Fast-flowing rocky streams, weirs, sometimes lakes and slow rivers. Winters more widely, even in towns.

☐ **CITRINE WAGTAIL** v E. Russia
Motacilla citreola Call a sharp *'tseep tseep'*. Habits like Yellow Wagtail. Looks very pale in winter. Asia most Eur. countries

☐ **WHITE WAGTAIL** (b) P △
Motacilla a. alba Shrill *'chizzik'*. Simple twittering song. Open country, farms, often near villages. Not always near water.

☐ *M. a. yarrelli*, Pied Wagtail R ● Britain Ireland

yarrelli

SWALLOWS: *Hirundinidae*   3:1 – 5:0

☐ **SAND MARTIN**   S p ● ↓
Riparia riparia Colonies nest in riverbanks and sandpits. Feeds mostly over water. Roost at night in reed-beds.

☐ **CRAG MARTIN**
Hirundo rupestris Breeds on cliffs, also buildings, often with House Martins. Nest is like the Swallow's.

☐ **SWALLOW**   S p ●
Hirundo rustica Cuplike mud nest inside farm buildings, also in suburbs. Pleasant twittering song a sign of spring.

☐ **RED-RUMPED SWALLOW**   v
Hirundo daurica Flight slower, more like House Martin's. Nest has a long entrance tunnel. Open country.

☐ **HOUSE MARTIN**   S p ●
Delichon urbica White rump. Slower, less swooping flight than Swallow's. Builds a closed mud nest under eaves.

SHRIKES: *Laniidae*   2:3 – 5:1

☐ **RED-BACKED SHRIKE**   S p ○ ↓↓
Lanius collurio Like all shrikes a songbird with the habits of a raptor. Drastically decreasing.

☐ **ISABELLINE SHRIKE**   v   SC Asia
Lanius isabellinus Paler, buffy, red-tailed. Similar habits.   Britain
Germany

☐ **LESSER GREY SHRIKE**   v ↓↓
Lanius minor Black across forehead. Pink-tinged underparts. Often hovers when hunting. Perches more upright.

☐ **GREAT GREY SHRIKE**   p w △
Lanius excubitor Large, long-tailed. The only shrike seen in winter.

meridion.

☐ *L. c. meridionalis*   —   S. France
Iberia

excub.

☐ **MASKED SHRIKE**   —
Lanius nubicus Pied. Perches less conspicuously.

☐ **WOODCHAT SHRIKE**   v ↓
Lanius senator Also pied, but chestnut crown and nape.

WAXWINGS: *Bombycillidae*   1:0 – 1:0

☐ **WAXWING**   p w △
Bombycilla garrulus Strong flight. Feeds in flocks on berries and buds. Irregular invasions.

DIPPERS: *Cinclidae*		1:0 – 1:0

☐ **DIPPER**   v
Cinclus c. cinclus   Hills with fast-running streams. Flies low and fast along the river course. Feeds under water.

☐ *C. c. gularis*   R w ●   S. E. Brit. Britanny

WRENS: *Troglodytidae*		1:0 – 1:0

☐ **WREN**   R p ●
Troglodytes troglodytes   Song loud and shrill for bird's tiny size. Solitary. In all kinds of vegetation.

☐ *T. t. zetlandicus*   R ◑   Shetland

☐ *T. t. hirtensis*   R ◑   St. Kilda

☐ *T. t. islandicus*   —   Iceland

ACCENTORS: *Prunellidae*		1:1 – 2:1

☐ **DUNNOCK**   R p ●
Prunella modularis   Or Hedge Sparrow. Thin bill. Bushes and shrubs everywhere, from gardens to high mountains.

☐ **ALPINE ACCENTOR**   v
Prunella collaris   High in mountains, lower only in winter. Hides behind rocks. Lark-like trilling song.

WARBLERS: *Sylviidae*		20:24 – 41:9

☐ **CETTI'S WARBLER**   R ○ ↑
Cettia cetti   More often heard than seen: loud explosive song. Overgrown ditches and marshes. Recent colonist in Britain.

☐ **FAN-TAILED WARBLER**   v
Cisticola juncidis   Tireless aerial song *'chip chip chip'*. Marshes, also cornfields and neglected grassland.

☐ **SAVI'S WARBLER**   S ○ ↑
Locustella luscinioides   Song like Grasshopper Warbler's. Reedy scrub. Unstreaked. Recolonising Britain, now *c.* 15 breeding pairs.

☐ **RIVER WARBLER**   v
Locustella fluviatilis   Wet, dense vegetation often in woods. Song like Grasshopper Warbler's, but more regular.

☐ **GRASSHOPPER WARBLER**   S ●
Locustella naevia   Sings like a cricket, from thick cover often minutes on end, day and night. Wet and dry habitats.

☐ **LANCEOLATED WARBLER**   v
Locustella lanceolata   More heavily streaked than Grasshopper Warbler. Similar song with whistling. Secretive.

tensis   *zetl.*

islandicus

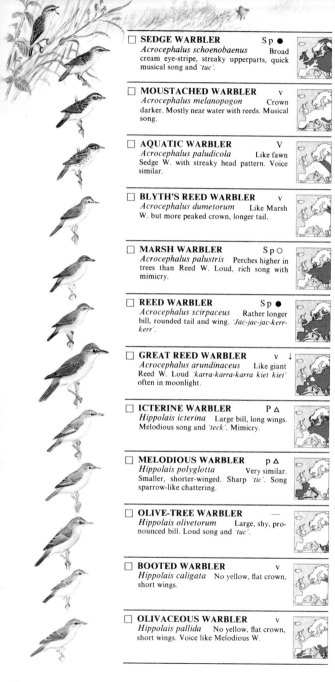

☐ **SEDGE WARBLER** Sp ●
Acrocephalus schoenobaenus Broad cream eye-stripe, streaky upperparts, quick musical song and *'tuc'*.

☐ **MOUSTACHED WARBLER** v
Acrocephalus melanopogon Crown darker. Mostly near water with reeds. Musical song.

☐ **AQUATIC WARBLER** V
Acrocephalus paludicola Like fawn Sedge W. with streaky head pattern. Voice similar.

☐ **BLYTH'S REED WARBLER** v
Acrocephalus dumetorum Like Marsh W. but more peaked crown, longer tail.

☐ **MARSH WARBLER** Sp ○
Acrocephalus palustris Perches higher in trees than Reed W. Loud, rich song with mimicry.

☐ **REED WARBLER** Sp ●
Acrocephalus scirpaceus Rather longer bill, rounded tail and wing. *'Jac-jac-jac-kerr-kerr'*.

☐ **GREAT REED WARBLER** v ↓
Acrocephalus arundinaceus Like giant Reed W. Loud *'karra-karra-karra kiet kiet'* often in moonlight.

☐ **ICTERINE WARBLER** P △
Hippolais icterina Large bill, long wings. Melodious song and *'teck'*. Mimicry.

☐ **MELODIOUS WARBLER** p △
Hippolais polyglotta Very similar. Smaller, shorter-winged. Sharp *'tic'*. Song sparrow-like chattering.

☐ **OLIVE-TREE WARBLER** —
Hippolais olivetorum Large, shy, pronounced bill. Loud song and *'tuc'*.

☐ **BOOTED WARBLER** v
Hippolais caligata No yellow, flat crown, short wings.

☐ **OLIVACEOUS WARBLER** v
Hippolais pallida No yellow, flat crown, short wings. Voice like Melodious W.

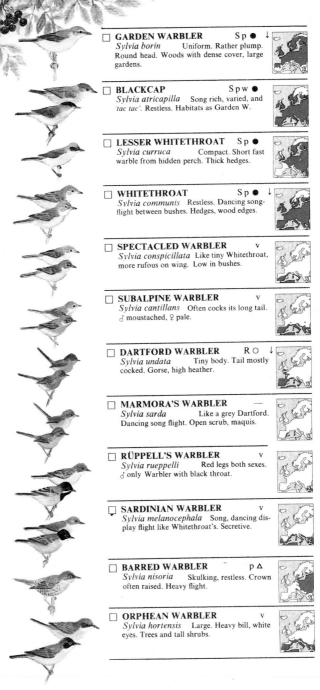

☐ **GARDEN WARBLER** S p ● ↓
Sylvia borin Uniform. Rather plump.
Round head. Woods with dense cover, large
gardens.

☐ **BLACKCAP** S p w ●
Sylvia atricapilla Song rich, varied, and
'tac tac'. Restless. Habitats as Garden W.

☐ **LESSER WHITETHROAT** S p ●
Sylvia curruca Compact. Short fast
warble from hidden perch. Thick hedges.

☐ **WHITETHROAT** S p ● ↓
Sylvia communis Restless. Dancing song-
flight between bushes. Hedges, wood edges.

☐ **SPECTACLED WARBLER** v
Sylvia conspicillata Like tiny Whitethroat,
more rufous on wing. Low in bushes.

☐ **SUBALPINE WARBLER** v
Sylvia cantillans Often cocks its long tail.
♂ moustached, ♀ pale.

☐ **DARTFORD WARBLER** R ○ ↓
Sylvia undata Tiny body. Tail mostly
cocked. Gorse, high heather.

☐ **MARMORA'S WARBLER** —
Sylvia sarda Like a grey Dartford.
Dancing song flight. Open scrub, maquis.

☐ **RÜPPELL'S WARBLER** v
Sylvia rueppelli Red legs both sexes.
♂ only Warbler with black throat.

☐ **SARDINIAN WARBLER** v
Sylvia melanocephala Song, dancing display flight like Whitethroat's. Secretive.

☐ **BARRED WARBLER** — p △
Sylvia nisoria Skulking, restless. Crown
often raised. Heavy flight.

☐ **ORPHEAN WARBLER** v
Sylvia hortensis Large. Heavy bill, white
eyes. Trees and tall shrubs.

43

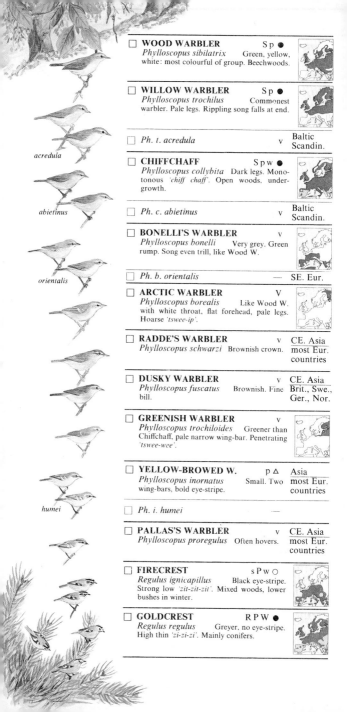

☐ **WOOD WARBLER**   Sp ●
Phylloscopus sibilatrix   Green, yellow, white: most colourful of group. Beechwoods.

☐ **WILLOW WARBLER**   Sp ●
Phylloscopus trochilus   Commonest warbler. Pale legs. Rippling song falls at end.

☐ *Ph. t. acredula*   v   Baltic Scandin.

acredula

☐ **CHIFFCHAFF**   Spw ●
Phylloscopus collybita   Dark legs. Monotonous *'chiff chaff'*. Open woods, undergrowth.

☐ *Ph. c. abietinus*   v   Baltic Scandin.

abietinus

☐ **BONELLI'S WARBLER**   v
Phylloscopus bonelli   Very grey. Green rump. Song even trill, like Wood W.

☐ *Ph. b. orientalis*   —   SE. Eur.

orientalis

☐ **ARCTIC WARBLER**   V
Phylloscopus borealis   Like Wood W. with white throat, flat forehead, pale legs. Hoarse *'tswee-ip'*.

☐ **RADDE'S WARBLER**   v   CE. Asia
Phylloscopus schwarzi   Brownish crown.   most Eur. countries

☐ **DUSKY WARBLER**   v   CE. Asia
Phylloscopus fuscatus   Brownish. Fine bill.   Brit., Swe., Ger., Nor.

☐ **GREENISH WARBLER**   v
Phylloscopus trochiloides   Greener than Chiffchaff, pale narrow wing-bar. Penetrating *'tswee-wee'*.

☐ **YELLOW-BROWED W.**   p △   Asia
Phylloscopus inornatus   Small. Two   most Eur. wing-bars, bold eye-stripe.   countries

☐ *Ph. i. humei*   —

humei

☐ **PALLAS'S WARBLER**   v   CE. Asia
Phylloscopus proregulus   Often hovers.   most Eur. countries

☐ **FIRECREST**   s P w ○
Regulus ignicapillus   Black eye-stripe. Strong low *'zit-zit-zit'*. Mixed woods, lower bushes in winter.

☐ **GOLDCREST**   R P W ●
Regulus regulus   Greyer, no eye-stripe. High thin *'zi-zi-zi'*. Mainly conifers.

FLYCATCHER: *Muscicapidae* 3:2 – 5:2

☐ **SPOTTED FLYCATCHER** S p ●
Muscicapa striata Perches upright, on bare look-out posts. Flicks tail, wings. Solitary, often near buildings.

☐ **PIED FLYCATCHER** S P ●
Ficedula hypoleuca Often changes perch or drops to ground. Flicks only one wing. Woods, orchards. Accepts nestboxes.

☐ **COLLARED FLYCATCHER** v
Ficedula albicollis Longer wings, white collar, rump. ♀ almost identical to Pied ♀. Habitat same.

☐ **HALF-COLLARED FLYC.** —
Ficedula semitorquata Like Collared F. but collar broken and more white in rump. Habitat as Pied F., also conifers.

☐ **RED-BREASTED FLYC.** p △
Ficedula parva Small, restless, keeps under cover, cocks tail. Low rattling *'chic'* and sad *'wee'*.

CHATS & THRUSHES: *Turdidae* 14:21 – 23:20

☐ **RED-FLANKED BLUETAIL** v
Tarsiger cyanurus Robin's shape, Redstart's habits, often on ground. Shy, often flicks tail. Dense, wet conifer forest.

☐ **NIGHTINGALE** S ● ↓
Luscinia megarhynchos Reddish-brown tail. Rich liquid song by day and night, with crescendo at end. Thick cover in dense broadleaved woods.

☐ **THRUSH-NIGHTINGALE** V
Luscinia luscinia Darker. Breast mottled. Louder song lacks final crescendo. Prefers wetter places. Interbreeds with Nightingale.

☐ **BLUETHROAT** (b) P △
Luscinia s. svecica Robin-like. Always with orange-red in tail. Shy. Bushes near water.

☐ *L. s. cyanecula* v central & south Europe

☐ **ROBIN** R s p w ●
Erithacus rubecula Round, neckless. Solitary. Gardens, shyer in woods. *'Tic tic'* and melancholy song, often in evening.

☐ **REDSTART** Sp ● ↓
Phoenicurus phoenicurus Robin-like, but seldom on ground. Solitary in trees. Clear warble and '*hweet-tuc-tuc*'.

☐ **BLACK REDSTART** SPw ○
Phoenicurus ochruros Darker. Male white in wings. Cliffs and buildings, often on ground. Scratchy warbling hiss.

☐ *Ph. o. aterrimus* Portugal SC. Spain

☐ **STONECHAT** Rs ●
Saxicola torquata Perches upright. Hard '*tsak-tsak*' like clinking stones.

☐ **WHINCHAT** Sp ● ↓
Saxicola rubetra Needs grassland with c. 1m high song posts. Imitates other birds.

☐ **WHEATEAR** Sp ●
Oenanthe o. oenanthe Conspicuous white in tail in flight. Mountains, rocky moors.

☐ *Oe. o. leucorrhoa* p △ Greenland Canada

☐ **ISABELLINE WHEATEAR** v
Oenanthe isabellina Like large ♀ Wheatear. Upright. Stony plains.

☐ **PIED WHEATEAR** v
Oenanthe pleschanka Slim, tail rather long. Often perches on shrubs.

☐ **DESERT WHEATEAR** Asia/N.Af.
Oenanthe deserti Tail mostly black. most Eur. countries

☐ **BLACK-EARED WHEATEAR** v
Oenanthe hispanica Variable but always rather pale-looking. Much white in tail.

☐ *Oe. h. melanoleuca* v Balk., Gr.

☐ **BLACK WHEATEAR** v
Oenanthe leucura Larger, more thrush-like. Black with white rump.

☐ **ROCK THRUSH** v
Monticola saxatilis Orange tail. Shy. Flies low. Jerks and flicks tail.

☐ **BLUE ROCK THRUSH** —
Monticola solitarius Looks black. Longish bill. Rocks, often old villages.

☐ **RUFOUS BUSH CHAT** v *Cercotrichas g. galactotes* Slim, rufous, cocks and fans white-tipped tail.	
☐ *C. g. syriacus* v	eastern
☐ **REDWING** r P W ○ *Turdus iliacus* Small. Bold eye-stripe, reddish flanks. Large winter flocks.	
☐ **SONG THRUSH** R P W ● *Turdus philomelos* Warm brown, spotted below. Loud varied song. Gardens, woodland.	
☐ **MISTLE THRUSH** R s ● *Turdus viscivorus* Bigger, boldly spotted. Greyer back, white underwing, tail tips.	
☐ **FIELDFARE** r P W ○ ↑ *Turdus pilaris* Grey rump, black tail. 'Chak-chak-chak' chatter. Wood edges, farm- land.	
☐ **RING OUZEL** S p ● *Turdus t. torquatus* Mountains. White wing-flash in flight. Hides behind rocks.	
☐ *T. t. alpestris* v	mountains of C & S Europe
☐ **BLACKBIRD** R P W ● ↑ *Turdus merula* ♀ often brownish with spotted breast. Town centres to wild uplands, where often shy.	
☐ **AMERICAN ROBIN** v *Turdus migratorius* Like a red-breasted Blackbird.	N. Amer. most Eur. countries
☐ **BLACK-THROATED THRUSH** V *Turdus ruficollis atrogularis* Dark with white belly.	Siberia most Eur. countries
☐ **EYE-BROWED THRUSH** v *Turdus obscurus* Like a pale Redwing. Unspotted breast.	Siberia most Eur. countries
☐ **OLIVE-BACKED THRUSH** v *Catharus ustulatus* Small. Spots on breast only.	N. Amer. most Eur. countries
☐ **SIBERIAN THRUSH** v *Zoothera sibirica* Underwing pattern.	Siberia most Eur. countries
☐ **WHITE'S THRUSH** v *Zoothera dauma* Large. 'Scaly' plumage.	Asia/Aust. all Europ. countries

alpestris

47

| **REEDLINGS:** *Panuridae* | 1:0 – 1:0 |

☐ **BEARDED TIT** R w ○
Panurus biarmicus Long-tailed, in reeds.
Weak flight. Metallic *'ping ping'*.

| **LONG-TAILED TITS:** *Aegithalidae* | 1:0 – 1:0 |

☐ **LONG-TAILED TIT** v
Aegithalos c. caudatus Long-tailed,
black + white. Often noisy parties. *'Tsirrup'*.

☐ *Ae. c. europaeus/rosaceus* R ● Contl./Brit.
☐ *"alpinus"* group — S. Europ.
countries

| **PENDULINE TITS:** *Remizidae* | 0:1 – 1:0 |

☐ **PENDULINE TIT** v ↑
Remiz pendulinus Tiny, restless. Fluttery
flight. Thin Robin-like *'tsee'*. Mostly near
water.

| **TITS:** *Paridae* | 6:0 – 9:0 |

☐ **SIBERIAN TIT** —
Parus cinctus Northern conifers and
birches.

☐ **MARSH TIT** R ●
Parus palustris *'Pitcheu'*, nasal *'tchay-
tchay'*, scolding *'chicka-bee-bee-bee'*. Song
clear *'schip'* 7 times.

☐ **WILLOW TIT** R ●
Parus montanus *'Erz-erz-erz'*, thin *'chi chi'*,
often with *'tchay tchay'*. Song sad *'piu piu piu'*.

☐ *P. m. borealis* v N. Scand.

☐ **SOMBRE TIT** —
Parus lugubris Large and drab.

☐ **CRESTED TIT** v
Parus cristatus Pine forests. Rolling
'prrrt prrrt'. Song *'chirr chirr chirrrr'*.

☐ *P. c. scoticus* R ◑ Scotland

☐ **BLUE TIT** R w ●
Parus caeruleus Acrobatic little blue bird.
Feeds on outer branches. Varied *'tsee-tsee-
tsee-tsit'*.

☐ **AZURE TIT** —
Parus cyanus Long tail, very white.

☐ **GREAT TIT** R w ●
Parus major Large. Bright white cheeks.
Finch-like *'pink'* and varied *'teecha-teecha-
teecha'*.

☐ **COAL TIT** v
Parus ater Smaller. White nape. Piping
musical *'tseu'*. Woods with conifers.

☐ *P. a. hibernicus/britannicus* R ● Irel./Brit.

borealis

scot.

NUTHATCHES: *Sittidae* 1:0 – 4:1

☐ **NUTHATCH** R ●
Sitta europaea caesia Often noisy *'chwit chwit'*. Always in trees, often head downwards.

☐ *S. e. europaea* — N. Europe

☐ **ROCK NUTHATCH** —
Sitta neumayer Paler. In rocky places.

☐ **CORSICAN NUTHATCH** —
Sitta whiteheadi Mountain conifers.

☐ **KRÜPER'S NUTHATCH** —
Sitta krueperi Conifer forests. Tit-like habits.

WALLCREEPERS: *Trichodromadidae* 0:1 – 1:0

☐ **WALLCREEPER** v
Trichodroma muraria Butterfly-like flight. Mountain cliffs, in winter lower, also buildings.

TREECREEPERS: *Certhiidae* 1:1 – 2:0

☐ **TREECREEPER** R ●
Certhia familiaris On trees. Thin song ends in trill *'tsee-tsee-tsit sissi-tsee'*.

☐ **SHORT-TOED TREECREEPER** v
Certhia brachydactyla Duller, rufous-tinged flanks. Louder *'titt didelidit'* song.

SPARROWS: *Passeridae* 2:1 – 5:0

☐ **HOUSE SPARROW** R ●
Passer d. domesticus Gregarious, always near humans, except groups visiting autumn cornfields.

☐ *P. d. italiae* — S. of the Alps (It.)

☐ **SPANISH SPARROWS** v
Passer hispaniolensis Brighter. Shrubs near river beds, sometimes villages.

☐ **TREE SPARROW** R ●
Passer montanus More open woodlands, field hedges. *'Tek tek'* flight note.

☐ **ROCK SPARROW** — ↓
Petronia petronia Stony ground, old towns. Loud *'tsweech'* and softer *'pitsch'*.

☐ **SNOW FINCH** —
Montifringilla nivalis High mountains. Often in ski resorts. Very white in tail and wing.

| **BUNTINGS:** *Emberizidae* | 7:19 – 14:18 |

☐ **CORN BUNTING**   R ● ↓
Miliaria calandra   Largest and drabbest bunting. Cultivated farmland. Sits on fences, wires. Song like rattling bunch of keys.

☐ **BLACK-HEADED BUNTING**   v
Emberiza melanocephala   Habits similar to Corn Bunting's, but colourful, unstreaked, more tuneful voice.

☐ **YELLOWHAMMER**   R ● ↓
Emberiza citrinella   Farmland, young conifers; stubble fields in winter. Song 'Little-bit-of-bread-and-no-cheese'.

☐ **PINE BUNTING**   v
Emberiza leucocephalos   Eastern   Sib./China
counterpart of Yellowhammer.   most Eur. countries

☐ **CIRL BUNTING**   R ○
Emberiza cirlus   Greenish-grey rump. Hedges, parks, gardens. Rattling song like Lesser Whitethroat's.

☐ **CINEREOUS BUNTING**   —
Emberiza cineracea   Dry rocky slopes. In Europe only on Lesbos and Chios. Typical bunting song.

☐ **ORTOLAN**   P △ ↓
Emberiza hortulana   In Britain migrants along coast, on Continent in fields, sometimes gardens.

☐ **CRETZSCHMAR'S BUNTING**   v
Emberiza caesia   Like Ortolan without yellow. Song similar. Dry rocky hills. Very tame.

☐ **ROCK BUNTING**   v
Emberiza cia   Mostly on dry hillsides from high mountains to sea-level. Bunting song with Dunnoch overtones. Wavering flight.

☐ **LITTLE BUNTING**   v
Emberiza pusilla   Small, like a female Reed Bunting. Call a hard, sharp 'zik'.

☐ **REED BUNTING**   R p w ● ↑
Emberiza schoeniclus   Wetland bird which is spreading to drier habitats, even cultivated fields. Abrupt, squeaky song.

☐ **RUSTIC BUNTING**   v
Emberiza rustica   Wet, northern forest edges. Robin-like song. In winter like Reed Bunting with chestnut rump.

☐ **YELLOW-BREASTED B.**   v
Emberiza aureola   Musical song like Ortolan's but quicker. Open country with bushes, mostly near water.

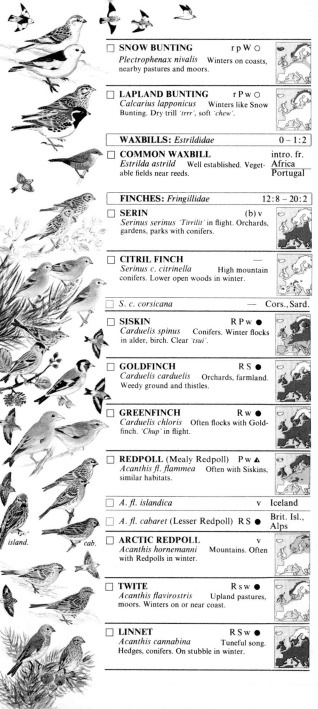

☐ **SNOW BUNTING** r p W ○
Plectrophenax nivalis Winters on coasts, nearby pastures and moors.

☐ **LAPLAND BUNTING** r P w ○
Calcarius lapponicus Winters like Snow Bunting. Dry trill *'trrr'*, soft *'chew'*.

WAXBILLS: *Estrildidae* 0 – 1:2

☐ **COMMON WAXBILL** intro. fr.
Estrilda astrild Well established. Veget- Africa
able fields near reeds. Portugal

FINCHES: *Fringillidae* 12:8 – 20:2

☐ **SERIN** (b) v
Serinus serinus 'Tirrilit' in flight. Orchards, gardens, parks with conifers.

☐ **CITRIL FINCH** —
Serinus c. citrinella High mountain conifers. Lower open woods in winter.

☐ *S. c. corsicana* — Cors., Sard.

☐ **SISKIN** R P w ●
Carduelis spinus Conifers. Winter flocks in alder, birch. Clear *'tsui'*.

☐ **GOLDFINCH** R S ●
Carduelis carduelis Orchards, farmland. Weedy ground and thistles.

☐ **GREENFINCH** R w ●
Carduelis chloris Often flocks with Gold-finch. *'Chup'* in flight.

☐ **REDPOLL** (Mealy Redpoll) P w ▲
Acanthis fl. flammea Often with Siskins, similar habitats.

☐ *A. fl. islandica* v Iceland

☐ *A. fl. cabaret* (Lesser Redpoll) R S ● Brit. Isl., Alps

☐ **ARCTIC REDPOLL** v
Acanthis hornemanni Mountains. Often with Redpolls in winter.

☐ **TWITE** R s w ●
Acanthis flavirostris Upland pastures, moors. Winters on or near coast.

☐ **LINNET** R S w ●
Acanthis cannabina Tuneful song. Hedges, conifers. On stubble in winter.

island. *cab.*

CROSSBILL
R W ◑
Loxia curvirostra Big head. *'Jip jip'* flight calls. Conifer woods, sometimes orchards.

SCOTTISH CROSSBILL
R ○
Loxia scotica Stronger bill. *'Joop joop'* in flight. Only in Scottish pinewoods.

PARROT CROSSBILL
V
Loxia pytyopsittacus Even larger bill, giving head weighty look. Deep *'jop jop'* in flight.

WHITE-WINGED CROSSBILL
v
Loxia leucoptera Slimmer, brighter. Two white wingbars. High *'jip jip'*, *'tjit tjit'*.

PINE GROSBEAK
v
Pinicola enucleator Large, longish. Stout body. Undulating flight. Narrow wingbars.

COMMON ROSEFINCH
v ↑
Carpodacus erythrinus Much smaller. Stout bill. ♀ sparrow-like. Woods, shrubs.

HAWFINCH
R p ●
Coccothraustes coccothraustes Not shy, but mostly high in trees. Quiet clicking *'psik'*. Parks, orchards and woods.

BULLFINCH
R w ● ↑
Pyrrhula pyrrhula Rump strikingly white in flight. Not shy but secretive, mostly in pairs. Low whistling *'deeu'*.

☐ *P. p. pyrrhula*	v	Scand.
☐ *P. p. iberiae*	—	Pyrenees N. Iberia

TRUMPETER FINCH
v
Bucanetes githagineus Voice like toy trumpet, nasal. Feeds on ground in stony uplands.

CHAFFINCH
R p W ●
Fringilla coelebs Perhaps our commonest bird. Call *'pink pink'*. Song loud clear *'chip chip chip chwee chwee tissi chooeeo'*.

BRAMBLING
P W (b) ▲
Fringilla montifringilla Rather harsh *'tsweek'*, in flight *'chucc chucc'*. Often large winter flocks when good beech mast.

pyrrhula   *iberia*

STARLINGS: *Sturnidae* 1:1 – 3:0

☐ **STARLING** R p W ● ↑
Sturnus vulgaris White-spotted all over in winter, when often huge quarrelsome roosts in reeds or on buildings or city trees.

☐ **SPOTLESS STARLING** —
Sturnus unicolor At distance looks like a Starling. Blacker. Song louder *'seuh'*.

☐ **ROSE-COLOURED STARLING** v
Sturnus roseus Gregarious. Often with Starlings. Forages in fields with cattle.

ORIOLES: *Oriolidae* 1:0 – 1:0

☐ **GOLDEN ORIOLE** s P ○
Oriolus oriolus Bright but very secretive, stays high in trees. Loud fluty *'weela weeo'*.

CROWS: *Corvidae* 7:1 – 11:1

Azure-winged Magpie

☐ **MAGPIE** R ●
Pica pica Only black + white bird perching in trees. Common everywhere except mountains.

☐ **AZURE-WINGED MAGPIE** —
Cyanopica cyana Gregarious, noisy. More woodland, esp. evergreen oaks, olive groves.

Siberian Jay

☐ **JAY** R w ●
Garrulus glandarius Common, noisy but secretive. White rump in flight. Woods, orchards, large hedges.

☐ **SIBERIAN JAY** —
Perisoreus infaustus Northern conifer forests. Tit-like habits. Not shy, but secretive in summer.

macrorh.

Chough

Alpine Chough

☐ **NUTCRACKER** —
Nucifraga c. caryocatactes Usually heard before seen – a harsh *'kraak'*. Likes hazelnuts, ripe fruit. Mainly conifer woods.

☐ *N. c. macrorhynchos* v Siberia
Irregular eruptions from east. all Eur. countries

☐ **CHOUGH** R ◉
Pyrrhocorax pyrrhocorax Mostly on sea cliffs in Britain. Buoyant aerobatic flight.

☐ **ALPINE CHOUGH** —
Pyrrhocorax graculus High mountain "crow" with tuneful finch-like whistling. Gregarious.

monedula

soemmerringii

☐ **JACKDAW** w △
Corvus m. monedula Small, short-billed, grey nape. Farmland, nests in tree holes and buildings.

☐ *C. m. spermologus* R ● Britain/
W. Eur.

☐ *C. m. soemmerringii* — S. Fin. to
Balk./Asia

spermologus

☐ **ROOK** R w ●
Corvus frugilegus Very gregarious whole year. Nesting colonies in trees. Winter flocks often mixed.

54

cornix

Hybrids: *corone* x *cornix*. Where
Carrion and Hooded meet, all
kinds of coloured hybrids occur.

☐ **CARRION CROW**   R w ●
Corvus c. corone   Commonest large black
bird in pairs or small flocks.

☐ **HOODED CROW**   R ●   Scot., E. &
C. c. cornix   SE. Eur.

☐ **Hybrids**
corone x *cornix*

☐ **RAVEN**   R ● ↓
Corvus corax   Largest.
Stout bill, wedge tail, strong
flight, soars and tumbles
in strong flight. Deep *'prruk'*.

Crows and Ravens often feed together on
the same carrion. They are difficult to tell
apart. Ravens are larger, bulkier, stronger
billed. When they fly, their cross-like
silhouette and wedge-shaped tail is typical.

Accidentals and Rare Vagrants

We list here species which have been recorded under 20 times in Europe. 'New' species are recorded in Europe almost every year. Southern or eastern species may overshoot their breeding grounds on migration, often in company with other species, or may get driven off-course by strong winds as are most American accidentals. Some even travel across the ocean on large ships. It is always highly exciting to see a 'new' bird, though to be officially accepted for one's national list, the record needs to be attested by several observers. Accidentals can occur almost anywhere, but islands off the coast are particularly good places.

This list excludes *aviary escapes* with two exceptions: the Chilean Flamingo which has bred in Germany; and the Red-headed Bunting, once very common in captivity and of which some records may have been natural occurrences.

Species on the British/Irish list are indicated with a v.

Pied-Billed Grebe	v	N/S Amer.	
Podilymbus podiceps		Britain	
Frigate Petrel	v	Atlantic Isl.	
Pelagodroma marina		Brit, Den	
Madeiran Petrel	v	Atl.Is, Port.	
Oceanodroma castro		Brit, Ire, Sp	
Wandering Albatross	–	S. Oceans	
Diomedea exulans		W.S.Eur.	
Yellow-Nosed Albatross	–	S. Oceans	
Diomedea chlororhynchos		Iceland	
Grey-Headed Albatross	–	S. Oceans	
Diomedea chrysostoma		Norway	
Light-Mantled Sooty Albatross	–	S. Oceans	
Phoebetria palpebrata		France	
Giant Petrel	–	S. Oceans	
Macronectes giganteus		Eng. Chan.	
Cape Petrel	v	S. oceans	
Daption capense		many	
Black-Capped Petrel	v	Caribbean	
Pterodroma hasitata		Britain	
Kermadec Petrel	v	S. Pacific	
Pterodroma neglecta		Britain	
Gould's Petrel	v	Pacific	
Pterodroma leucoptera		Wales	
Audubon's Petrel	v?	W. Atlantic	
Puffinus lherminieri		Britain?	
Bulwer's Petrel	v	Atlantic Isl.	
Bulweria bulwerii		Sp, Brit, Ire	
Jouanin's Petrel	–	Ind. Ocean	
Bulweria fallax		Italy	
Magnificent Frigatebird	v	S. Atlantic	
Fregata magnificens		Fr, Scot	
Least Bittern	v	America	
Ixobrychus exilis		Ireland	
Shrencks' Little Bittern	–	E. Asia	
Ixobrychus eurhythmus		It, Ger	
Green Heron	–	Am, Af, As	
Butorides striatus		esc.? Brit	
Chinese Pond Heron	–	E. Asia	
Ardeola bacchus		Norway	
Reef Heron	–	Africa	
Egretta gularis		Fr, Yu	
Bald Ibis	–	Moroc, Tur	
Geronticus eremita		Spain	
Lesser Flamingo	–	Africa	
Phoenicopterus minor		Spain	
Chilean Flamingo	–	south S.Am	
Phoenicopterus chilensis		esc. Ger	
White-Faced Tree Duck	–	Af, S.Am	
Dendrocygna viduata		Spain	
Black Duck	–	N. America	
Anas rubripes		Ire, Brit, It	
Falcated Duck	all esc.?	N.E. Asia	
Anas falcata		Sw, Fr, Cz, Aus	

Canvasback	–	N. America	
Aythya valisineria		Britain	
Bufflehead	v	N. America	
Bucephala albeola		Ice, Brit, Cz	
Hooded Merganser	v	N. America	
Mergus cucullatus		Ire, Brit	
Lappet-Faced Vulture	–	Af./W. As	
Torgos tracheliotus		Italy	
Bald Eagle	v	N. America	
Haliaeetus leucocephalus		Wales	
Pallas's Fish Eagle	–	N. Asia	
Haliaeetus leucoryphus		many	
Chanting Goshawk	–	Africa	
Melierax metabates		Sp, Gr	
Swallow-Tailed Kite	–	America	
Elanoides forificatus esc. ?		Fr, Ger	
Sooty Falcon	–	N.E. Africa	
Falco concolor		Italy	
American Kestrel	v	America	
Falco sparverius		Brit, Den	
Sandhill Crane	v. esc. ?	N. America	
Grus canadensis		Ireland	
Siberian Crane	–	Asia	
Grus leucogeranus		Sweden	
Allen's Gallinule	–	Africa	
Porphyrula alleni		many	
Am. Purple Gallinule	v	America	
Porphyrula martinica		Scilly	
Sora	v	N. America	
Porzana carolina		Brit, Fr	
White-Tailed Plover	v	Asia	
Chettusia leucura		Brit, Fr	
Semipalmated Plover	v	N. America	
Charadrius semipalmatus		Scilly	
Kittlitz's Plover	–	Africa	
Charadrius pecuarius		Norway	
Lesser Sandplover	v	Asia	
Charadrius mongolus		N. Europe?	
Greater Sandplover	v	S. Asia	
Charadrius leschenaultii		Gr, Sw, Ger, Brit	
Caspian Plover old rec	v	Asia	
Charadrius asiaticus		Helgo, It, Bul, Brit	
Short-Billed Dowitcher	v	N. America	
Limnodromus griseus		Brit,Fr,Ger, Nor, Den	
Little Whimbrel	–	Asia	
Numenius minutus		N. Europe?	
Hudsonian Godwit	v?	Canada	
Limosa haemastica		Britain	
Willet	–	N. America	
Catoptophorus semipalmatus		Fr, Sw, Yu	
Wandering Tattler	v?	NW N.Am	
Heteroscelus incanus		Britain	

☐ **Red-Necked Stint**	–	N. Sib/Alas
Calidris ruficollis		Germany
☐ **Long-Toed Stint**	–	Asia
Calidris subminuta		Sweden
☐ **Senegal Thick-knee**	–	Africa
Burhinus senegalensis		Italy?
☐ **White-Eyed Gull**	–	Africa
Larus leucophthalmus		Greece
☐ **Grey-Headed Gull**	–	Af/S. Am
Larus cirrocephalus		S. Spain
☐ **Franklin's Gull**	v	N. America
Larus pipixan		Brit, Fr
☐ **Royal Tern**	v	W. Africa, W. Indies
Sterna maxima		S.W. N. Eu
☐ **Forster's Tern**	v	N. America
Sterna forsteri		Ice, Brit
☐ **Aleutian Tern**	v	N. Pacific
Sterna aleutica		Britain
☐ **Bridled Tern**	v	Tropics
Sterna anaethetus		Britain
☐ **Brown Noddy**	–	Trop. Ocns
Anous stolidus		Germany
☐ **Parakeet Auklet**	–	N. Pacific
Cyclorrhynchus psittacula		Sweden
☐ **Crested Auklet**	–	N. Pacific
Aethia cristatella		Iceland
☐ **Spotted Sandgrouse**	–	Afro-Asian
Pterocles senegallus		Italy
☐ **Chestnut-Bellied Sandgrouse**	–	Africa
Pterocles exustus		Hungary
☐ **Rufous Turtle Dove**	v	Asia
Streptopelia orientalis		many
☐ **Jacobin Cuckoo**	–	Afro-Asian
Clamator jacobinus		Finland
☐ **Black-Billed Cuckoo**	–	N. America
Coccyzus erythropthalmus		many
☐ **African Marsh Owl**	–	Africa
Asio capensis		Sp, Port
☐ **Egyptian Nightjar**	–	Near East, N. Africa
Caprimulgus aegyptius		many
☐ **Common Nightjar**	v	N. America
Chordeiles minor		Ice, Brit
☐ **Needle-Tailed Swift**	–	Asia
Hirundapus caudacutus		It, Fin, Brit
☐ **Little Swift**	v	Af, S. Asia
Apus affinus		It, Ire
☐ **Pacific Swift**	v	Asia
Apus pacificus		Britain
☐ **Pied Kingfisher**	–	Af, S.Asia
Ceryle rudis		Gr, Pol
☐ **Belted Kingfisher**	v	N. America
Ceryle alcyon		Ire, Brit, Neth, Ice
☐ **White-Breasted Kingfisher**	–	Asia
Halcyon smyrnensis		Greece
☐ **Blue-Cheeked Bee-Eater**	v	Afro-Asian
Merops superciliosus		many
☐ **Yellow-Bellied Sapsucker**	v	N. America
Sphyrapicus varius		Scilly, Ice
☐ **Acadian Flycatcher**	–	N. America
Empidonax virescens		Iceland
☐ **Indian Sandlark**	–	S. Asia
Calandrella raytal		Spain
☐ **Bar-Tailed Desert Lark**	–	Afro-Asian
Ammomanes cincturus		Malta
☐ **Desert Lark**	–	Afro-Asian
Ammomanes deserti		Spain
☐ **Hoopoe Lark**	–	N. Africa, Near East
Alaemon alaudipes		Malta
☐ **Bimaculated Lark**	v	Near East, W. Siberia
Melanocorypha bimaculata		Fin, Brit, It
☐ **Blyth's Pipit**	v	E. Asia
Anthus godlewskii		Brit, Fin
☐ **American Pipit**	v	Greenland, N. America
Anthus spinoletta rubescens		Britain
☐ **Common Bulbul**	–	Afro-Asian
Pycnonotus barbatus		Spain
☐ **Brown Thrasher**	v	N. America
Toxostoma rufum		Britain
☐ **Cat Bird**	v	N. America
Dumetella carolinensis		Brit, Heligo
☐ **Siberian Accentor**	–	N. Asia
Prunella montanella		widely
☐ **Gray's Grasshopper Warbler**	–	Asia
Locustella fasciolata		Fr, Den
☐ **Pallas's Grasshopper Warbler**	v	Siberia
Locustella certhiola		Brit, Ire, Neth, Heligo
☐ **Paddyfield Warbler**	v	S.Rus, Asia
Acrocephalus agricola		most Eur. countries
☐ **Thick-Billed Warbler**	v	N. Asia
Acrocephalus aedon		Britain
☐ **Desert Warbler**	v	N. Africa, Near East
Sylvia nana		many
☐ **Ménétries' Warbler**	–	Mid. East
Sylvia mystacea		Greece
☐ **Tristram's Warbler**	–	Africa
Sylvia deserticola		Spain
☐ **Green Warbler**	–	Asia
Phylloscopus nitidus		Heligoland
☐ **Brown Flycatcher**	v	E. Asia
Muscicapa latirostris		Brit, Den, Nor, Faer
☐ **Mugimaki Flycatcher**	–	E. Asia
Ficedula mugimaki		Italy
☐ **Narcissus Flycatcher**	–	E. Asia
Ficedula narcissina		France
☐ **Siberian Rubythroat**	v	N. Asia
Luscinia calliope		Ice, Brit, Fr, It
☐ **Siberian Blue Robin**	v	E. Asia
Luscinia cyane		Sark
☐ **White-Throated Robin**	–	Mid. East
Irania gutturalis		Sweden
☐ **Moussier's Redstart**	–	Africa
Phoenicurus moussieri		Sp, Malta
☐ **White-Crowned Black Wheatear**	–	N. Africa
Oenanthe leucopyga		Malta

☐ **Naumann's Thrush**	v Siberia		☐ **Rufous-Sided Towhee**	v N. America
Turdus n. naumanni	most Eur. countries		*Pipilo erythrophalmus*	Britain
☐ *T.n. eunomus*, Dusky Thrush	C. Europe		☐ **Savannah Sparrow**	– N. America
			Ammodramus sandwichensis	Britain
☐ *Turdus r. ruficollis*, Red-Throated Thrush	Siberia Germany		☐ **Fox Sparrow**	v N. America
			Zonotrichia iliaca	Britain
☐ **Tickell's Thrush**	– Himalaya		☐ **Song Sparrow**	v N. America
Turdus unicolor	Heligoland		*Zonotrichia melodia*	Britain
☐ **Wood Thrush**	– N. America		☐ **White-Crowned Sparrow**	v N. America
Hylocichla mustelina	Iceland		*Zonotrichia leucophrys*	Fr, Shet. Britain
☐ **Hermit Thrush**	v N. America		☐ **White-Throated Sparrow**	v N. America
Catharus guttatus	Shet, Ger		*Zonotrichia albicollis*	Den, Brit
☐ **Veery**	v N. America		☐ **Lark Sparrow**	v N. America
Catharus fuscescens	Britain		*Chondestes grammacus*	Britain
☐ **Grey-Cheeked Thrush**	v N. America		☐ **Slate-Coloured Junco**	v N. America
Catharus minimus	Britain		*Junco hyemalis*	Brit, Ire
☐ **Red-Breasted Nuthatch**	– N. America		☐ **Black-Faced Bunting**	– N. Asia
Sitta canadensis	Iceland		*Emberiza spodocephala*	Heligoland
☐ **Red-Eyed Vireo**	v N. America		☐ **Siberian Meadow Bunting**	v N. Asia
Vireo olivaceus	Brit, Ger		*Emberiza cioides*	Brit, It
☐ **Black-and-White Warbler**	v N. America		☐ **Yellow-Browed Bunting**	v Siberia
Mniotilta varia	Brit, It, Ire		*Emberiza chrysophrys*	Bel, Fr, Britain
☐ **Tennessee Warbler**	v N. America		☐ **White-Capped Bunting**	– Asia
Vermivora peregrina	Ice, Brit		*Emberiza stewarti*	Belgium
☐ **Parula Warbler**	v N. America		☐ **Chestnut Bunting**	– N.E. Asia
Parula americana	Ice, Brit		*Emberiza rutila*	Nor, Neth, Fr
☐ **Yellow Warbler**	v N. America		☐ **Palla's Reed Bunting**	v N. Asia
Dendroica petechia	Britain		*Emberiza pallasi*	Brit, Den
☐ **Cape May Warbler**	v N. America		☐ **Red-Headed Bunting**	esc. ? v Asia
Dendroica tigrina	Scotland			esc. ? most European countries
☐ **Black-Throated Green Warbler**	v N. America		*Emberiza bruniceps*	
Dendroica virens	Heligoland		☐ **Bobolink**	v N. America
☐ **Magnolia Warbler**	v N. America		*Dolichonyx oryzivorus*	Brit, Ire
Dendroica magnolia	Britain		☐ **Northern Oriole**	v N. America
☐ **Palm Warbler**	v N. America		*Icterus galbula*	Ice, Brit
Dendroica palmarum	Britain		☐ **Black-Vented Oriole**	– Mexico
☐ **Myrtle Warbler**	v N. America		*Icterus wagleri*	Norway
Dendroica coronata	Ire, Brit		☐ **Yellow-Headed Blackbird**	– N. America
☐ **Black Poll Warbler**	v N. America		*X. xanthocephalus*	Den, Sw
Dendroica striata	Ire, Brit		☐ **Red-Billed Firefinch**	Africa
☐ **American Redstart**	v N. America		*Lagonosticta senegala*	esc. Spain
Setophaga ruticilla	Fr, Brit		☐ **Crimson-Rumped Waxbill**	– Africa
☐ **Ovenbird**	v N. America		*Estrilda rhodopyga*	esc. Spain
Seirus aurocapillus	Ire, Shet		☐ **Pallas's Rosefinch**	– Siberia
☐ **Northern Waterthrush**	v N. America		*Carpodacus roseus*	Hungary
Seirus noveboracensis	Scilly, Fr		☐ **Evening Grosbeak**	v N. America
☐ **Yellowthroat**	v N. America		*Hesperiphona vespertina*	Britain
Geothlypis trichas	Britain		☐ **Daurian Jackdaw**	– Sib, China
☐ **Hooded Warbler**	v N. America		*Corvus dauuricus*	Finland
Wilsonia citrina	Scilly		☐	
☐ **Wilson's Warbler**	v N. America			
Wilsonia pusilla	Britain		☐	
☐ **Summer Tanager**	v N. America			
Piranga rubra	Britain		☐	
☐ **Scarlet Tanager**	v N. America			
Piranga olivacea	Ire, Britain			
☐ **Indigo Bunting**	– N. America			
Passerina cyanea	Ice, Britain			
☐ *P. c. amoena*, Lazuli Bunting	– N. America Brit, Nor			
☐ **Rose-Breasted Grosbeak**	v N. America			
Pheucticus ludovicianus	Britain			

Index of English Names

62